IMAGES OF WAR

ALLIED BOMBING RAIDS: HITTING BACK AT THE HEART OF GERMANY

RARE PHOTOGRAPHS FROM WARTIME ARCHIVES

PHILIP KAPLAN

Pen & Sword
AVIATION

First printed in Great Britain in 2014 by
Pen & Sword Aviation
an imprint of
Pen & Sword Books Ltd.
47 Church Street
Barnsley,
South Yorkshire
S70 2AS

A CIP record for this book is available from the British Library.

ISBN 978 1 78346 289 6

Printed and bound in England
By CPI Group (UK) Ltd. Croydon, CR0 4YY

Pen & Sword Books Ltd incorporates the Imprints of Pen & Sword Aviation, Pen & Sword Family History, Pen & Sword Maritime, Pen & Sword Military, Pen & Sword Discovery, Wharncliffe Local History, Wharncliffe True Crime, Wharncliffe Transport, Pen & Sword Select, Pen & Sword Military Classics, Leo Cooper, The Praetorian Press, Remember When, Seaforth Publishing and Frontline Publishing.

For a complete list of Pen & Sword titles please contact Pen & Sword Books Limited
47 Church Street, Barnsley, South Yorkshire, S70 2AS, England

E-mail: enquiries@pen-and-sword.co.uk
Website: www.pen-and-sword.co.uk

Contents

DOING IT IN BROAD DAYLIGHT   3
ALLIES   11
GETTING UP FOR A MISSION   21
KEY TARGETS   30
TAKE-OFF AND ASSEMBLY   43
BASE ROUTINE   52
WAR IN THE AIR   66
HOME SWEET HOME   90
AN AMERICAN RAID   101
ON THE NOSE   114

The author is grateful to the following for the use of their published and/or unpublished material, or for their kind assistance in the preparation of this book: Fred Allen, John Archer, Roger A. Armstrong, Beth and David Alston, Eric Barnard, Malcolm Bates, Mike Benarcik, Robert Best, Ron Bicker, Larry Bird, Quentin Bland, Charles Bosshardt, Sam Burchell, Leonard Cheshire, Paul Chryst, Jack Clift, Jack Currie (for his text) Jim Dacey, E.W. Deacon, James H. Doolittle, Lawrence Drew, Ira Eakin, Gary Eastman, Gilly Fielder, W.W. Ford, Alan Foreman, Carsten Fries, Bill Ganz, Stephen Grey, Roland Hammersley, Ian Hawkins, Dave Hill, Franc Isla, Claire and Joe Kaplan, Neal Kaplan, Margaret Kaplan, Paul Kemp, Percy Kindred, Nick Kosiuk, Edith Kup, William T. Larkins, Robert D. Loomis, David C. Lustig, Donald Maffett, Ella Mayhew, Dickie Mayes, Cheryl and Mike Mathews, Tilly McMaster, Frank Nelson, Keith Newhouse, Michael O'Leary, Merle Olmsted, Tony Partridge, Colin Paterson, John Pawsey, L.W. Pilgrim, Reg Payne, Douglas Radcliffe, Sidney Rapoport, Lynn Ray, Duane Reed, Alan Reeves, Ted Richardson, Kay Riley, Dave Shelhamer, Paul Sink, Dale O. Smith, Tony Starcer, James Stewart, Ken Stone, Lloyd Stovall, Calvin Swaffer, John Thomas, Leonard Thompson, Albert Tyler, Robert White, Ray Wild, Jack Woods, Dennis Wrynn, Sam Young. Reasonable efforts have been made to trace copyright holders to use their material. The author apologizes for any omissions. All reasoale efforts will be made to correct such omissions in future editions.

Doing It in Broad Daylight

In 1942, when Brigadier General Ira C. Eaker of the United States Army Air Force stepped down from his Dakota at Hendon airport in beleaguered Britain, the war news was as bleak as the February weather. Japanese forces had invaded Singapore, their torpedo planes had sunk two major British battleships, the Americans were making a last stand on Bataan, the Allied armies were retreating across the plains of Libya, the Wehrmacht's Panzer tanks were closing in on Stalingrad, and Atlantic shipping losses to the predatory U-boats were frighteningly high. That very week, the warships *Scharnhorst, Gneisenau,* and *Prinz Eugen* had made a dash through the English Channel from their vulnerable anchorages in Brest harbor and had reached the safety of a German port. Desperate attempts by the RAF and the Fleet Air Arm had failed to stop them, and critics of air power wanted to know why; recent operations by RAF bombers, restricted by weather, had been relatively modest. British disciples of aerial bombardment were having a hard time.

Two events, however, held some promise of better days to come: one, Eaker's mission to prepare the way for the arrival of the U.S. Eighth Air Force; two, the RAF's bomber force had a new commander in the redoubtable Air Chief Marshal Arthur T. Harris who had established his headquarters on the hill above High Wycombe.

The early signs, however, were not encouraging. Eight weeks after Eaker's arrival, the two

The crew of the B-17 *Jersey Jinx* after a misson to Germany.

RAF squadrons then equipped with Avro Lancasters were assigned to attack the great M.A.N. factory in Augsburg, Bavaria, where the U-boats' diesel engines were being made. The concept of mounting a deep penetration raid in daylight was audacious—as audacious in its way as the attack, hours later, by Colonel Jimmy Doolittle's carrier-launched force of B-25 bombers on targets in Japan. The thinking at High Wycombe was that the new four-engined bombers, flying at low level in two elements of six, stood a good chance of success, and certainly a better chance than the lightly armed Wellingtons, underpowered Manchesters, and lumbering Stirlings that formed the bulk of Harris's command, but so much depended on the achievement of surprise. That essential element was lost when, by miscalculation, the first six Lancasters crossed a Luftwaffe fighter field on their passage over France, and four of them were shot down by Me 109s. A fifth was destroyed by flak above the target, as were two of the following element. Only five aircraft, two of which were badly damaged, struggled back to England on that April evening. John Nettleton, their leader, was awarded the Victoria Cross, Britain's highest military distinction. There was no lack of heroism, and no lack of skill (the factory was struck by thirteen one-thousand-pounders), but there was a fatal lack of firepower. The Lancaster's eight machine-guns, firing .303 bullets, had been no match for the cannons of the Me 109s.

It so happened, soon after his arrival, that Eaker had visited Harris's headquarters. The two men had worked together in Washington when Harris led a mission there in 1941, and it was as a friend that the American now sought the Englishman's assistance and advice. Eaker was an advocate of precision bombing, essentially in daylight, by well-armed aircraft flying in tight formation, whereas Harris's usual practice was to send his heavy bombers individually by night, making up for the inevitable loss of accuracy by sheer weight of numbers.

After one or two attempts to persuade the American to "come in with us on the night offensive," and a jocular suggestion that Eaker's reluctance was due to the fact that his airmen could only navigate in daylight, Harris accepted Eaker's point. He postponed the formation of a new RAF bomber group (later to emerge as the Pathfinder Force) to provide the Americans with bases in the Midlands and East Anglia. In addition the RAF found a fine old

far left: USAAF General Ira Eaker, 1942; Air Chief Marshal Arthur Harris, head of RAF Bomber Command; centre: RAF Wellington bombers; above: An Avro Manchester, forerunner of the Avro Lancaster bomber; left: A Bristol-engined Lancaster, the great majority of Lancs were Rolls-Royce or Packard Merlin-powered aircraft.

building for the Eighth Air Force bomber staff at nearby Daw's Hill Lodge, another for the fighter staff at Bushey Hall near Watford and, more importantly, gave the Americans access to a tried and tested nationwide system of communications and control.

An official U.S. record described how the Eighth Air Force was received: "With its Fighter Command guarding the skies by day, the Bomber Command striking the enemy by night, and the Coastal Command sweeping the sea-lanes, the RAF might have taken a condescending attitude towards the advance guard of Americans whose plans were so large and whose means were apparently so small. The RAF took no such attitude. From the start, their generous and sympathetic interest were the keys that unlocked many problems. 'Tell us what you want,' they said. 'If we have it, it is yours.' They might have added, 'Whether or not we need it ourselves.' "

The efficient organization of supplies was crucial to the operation, and it was undertaken by one of Eaker's staff, Major Frederick Castle, whose subsequent career as a combat leader was to add a page of glory to the story of the Eighth; USAAF intelligence officers attended briefings and debriefings at RAF bomber fields; technicians took note of the comments made by British airmen on certain operational shortcomings in the early Flying Fortresses and ordered the appropriate improvements. The Americans were welcomed everywhere they went. At a dinner in his honor, Eaker's speech was short and to the point: "We won't do much talking until we've done more flying. We hope that when we leave, you'll be glad we came. Thank you."

below: A Short Stirling is fueled and bombed up at its hardstand; right: The B-17, *Yankee Doodle*, lead ship of the first USAAF bombing mission of the war in Europe.

In the azure mid-afternoon of August 17, 1942, twelve B-17s of the 97th Bomb Group set out from Grafton Underwood on the first Eighth Air Force mission of the war. Taking off at thirty-second intervals, the aircraft climbed up into a sunlit, cloudless sky. Ira Eaker, as commanding general, flew in *Yankee Doodle*, leading the second element of six. The target, appositely, was the railway marshaling yard in Rouen, the city where five hundred years before, Joan of Arc had died for the liberty of France. Eighteen tons of bombs were dropped from 22,500 feet, and all fell on or near the target. None of the bombers (which the Germans identified as Lancasters) suffered more than superficial damage. Their escort of RAF Spitfires, two of which were lost, destroyed two Messerschmitts and claimed five more as 'probables.' When the B-17s returned to Grafton Underwood at seven o'clock that evening, the first to land was *Yankee Doodle*, as was right and proper. A message from Harris was brought to Ira Eaker: "Yankee Doodle certainly went to town, and can stick yet another well-earned feather in his cap."

The weather stayed fine and the 97th flew three more short-range missions with no losses to the bombers. Then, on August 21, nine B-17s en route to Rotterdam were late for the rendezvous with their fighter escort, and the Spitfires, short of fuel, were obliged to leave them halfway to the target. A recall was broadcast later, but for twenty minutes the German fighter pilots had the bombers to themselves. In the ensuing combat, the Fortress gunners claimed to have destroyed two fighters and to have damaged five, but one straggling bomber, attacked by five Fw 190s, was lucky to escape with one man wounded and another dying. It was a salutary engagement.

below: Messerschmitt Bf 109s, mainstay fighter of the German Air Force through much of the Second World War; right: An American attack on the U-boat pen facilities at La Pallice on the Brittany coast of France.

The Consolidated B-24 Liberators entered the arena on October 9, when the 93rd Bomb Group joined the 97th in an attack on steelworks and locomotive factories in Lille. There were a number of 'abortives,' with bombs dropped in the Channel, and only sixty-nine of 108 bombers reached the primary target. Nevertheless, it was the heaviest raid yet mounted by the Eighth, a distinction that it would hold, for one reason or another, for the next six months. It was also the first time the bombers had tangled with the Luftwaffe in force. As one navigator put it: "Lille was our first real brawl." In over two hundred combats the enemy fighters only succeeded in shooting down four bombers, but the skill and ferocity demonstrated by the German pilots gave notice of what might be expected in the days to come. Although enthusiastic claims of over sixty enemy aircraft certainly or probably destroyed were greeted with caution by the debriefing officers and subsequently reduced to forty-two, the figures still showed that the gunners in the well-named Flying Fortresses could give a good account of themselves.

The flak above the target was described by a Liberator crewman as "the worst I've ever seen." The fact that he was flying his first mission detracted a little from the force of his remark, but ensured its remembrance in the annals of the group. Three aircraft were shot down by flak, and twenty-two were damaged.

In November 1942, tactics were still in the process of evolving when, seeking greater accuracy, thirty-one B-17s attacked the U-boat pens at St Nazaire from less than half their norma

bombing height. Three aircraft were shot down by flak, and twenty-two were damaged. There were no more medium-altitude attacks by heavy bombers. The the 305th Bomb Group commander, Colonel Curtis E. LeMay, decided to abandon individual bomb runs: his squadrons would fly in train above the target, and each plane's bombs would be dropped when the leader's load began to fall. Two months later, St Nazaire was once again the target when LeMay's method was employed. The results were encouraging: more bombs fell near the MPI, the mean point of impact of an ideal strike. Bomb-on-the-leader tactics had been tried and proven.

When Ray Wild arrived at Podington to join the 92nd Bomb Group, one of his first actions was to look up an RAF pilot who had been a classmate during training in the States. "He and I went out," said Wild, "and had a couple of beers with some of his buddies. They felt that we Americans were out of our minds. They had tried daylight bombing and it just wasn't feasible. They said we'd get the hell shot out of us. They were right: on the first few raids we did get the hell shot out of us. But those Limeys did something that sure would scare me—night bombing. They'd come in over a target a minute apart, one guy this way, another guy from another point in the compass. This would scare me to death. They had tremendous intestinal fortitude. They were also realistic in that they couldn't bomb by daylight. Those Lancs were built to carry bombs, and not to protect themselves, while we could. So long as we stayed in tight formation, we could throw a lot of lead out in the right direction at the right time."

By the time spring came to England in 1943, several lessons had been learned, most of them the hard way. By now, every Eighth Air Force crewman knew that, to the Luftwaffe, the sight of a crippled airplane or a straggler, was like the taste of blood to a school of piranha. On future missions, the bombers would fly in combat box formations of lead, high, and low squadrons, planned to provide the maximum defensive firepower. At the IP (initial point), some miles from the target, the squadrons would move into line astern, bomb with the lead planes, and reform at a rally point for the homeward flight.

Both the Allied bomber force commanders now had a number of twin-engine planes at their disposal. The Eighth had formed a group of B-26 Martin Marauders, and would soon form more, while the RAF Bomber Command was being reinforced by squadrons of de Havilland Mosquitoes. The heavily-armed, six-man crew Marauders, flying in two boxes of eighteen airplanes each, would attack the industrial targets in France and the low-countries with one-ton loads of bombs; the versatile Mosquitoes, crewed by a pilot and a navigator, unarmed but flying higher and faster than any twin piston-engine aircraft yet conceived, were being increasingly used as pathfinders by the RAF, and by the Eighth for photo reconnaissance; as Harris's Light Night Striking Force, they would eventually carry two-ton "cookies" to Berlin on four nights out of six.

Eaker and Harris were agreed: between them they would wield a rapier by day and a bludgeon by night, and 1943 would be a big year for the bombers.

left: A de Havilland Mosquito, the "wooden wonder," for its unique construction type. It served in many roles, as a bomber, fighter-bomber, night fighter, maritime strike aircraft, as well as photo reconnaissance; right: Regulars of the Woodman pub on the edge of the American air base at Nuthampstead, Herts., with airmen of the USAAF in 1944.

Allies

"The enemy must be attacked by day and by night," announced Sir Archibald Sinclair, the British Air Secretary, "so that he may have no respite from the Allied blows, so that his defensive resources may be taxed to the utmost limit. But day and night bombing are separate though complementary tasks. Each requires a strategic plan, a tactical execution and a supporting organization adapted to its special needs. So there has been a division of labour. To one force—the Eighth Bomber Command—has been allotted the task of day bombing. To the other force—our Bomber Command—the task of night bombing. The methods are different, but the aim is the same: to paralyze the armed forces of Germany by disrupting the war economy by which they are sustained."

The civil servant who prepared those phrases for his minister had no need to pull his punches. In the year just passed, bombing policy had changed. The RAF's attacks were no longer restricted to "military targets," and gone were the days when only propaganda leaflets could be dropped on cities. The early German air attacks on Warsaw, Rotterdam, Coventry, and London had shown what could be done, and Britain's mood was hardened. "They have sown the wind,: said Air Chief Marshal Harris, "now they will reap the whirlwind."

Initially, there had been little difference in the way the bomber tactics of the Luftwaffe and the RAF evolved. Both had begun with daylight raids—the Germans on what then had seemed a massive scale—both had suffered heavy losses from the other's air defenses, and both had been obliged to seek the cover of the night. It was in the way the opposing forces developed and conducted their night operations that the differences emerged. A major factor was that the German aircraft industry was never able to provide the Luftwaffe with an effective heavy bomber, whereas the British airplane designers, responding to the RAF's requirement, produced the huge four-engined Short Stirling, the Handley-Page Halifax, and, at last, the Avro Lancaster. Then, to find their targets, the German crews depended on visual checkpoints such as estuaries and rivers, or, when bombing through the overcast, by flying along a radio beam transmitted from Europe; the RAF, meanwhile, was developing radar navigation and all-weather methods of pyrotechnic target-marking.

The main contrast, however, between the two offensives was in their weight and scale. While the Eighth's day offensive was gathering momentum, and Harris's new heavies flew in growing numbers to pound industrial targets deep inside the Reich, the German raids dwindled until they could be regarded, strategically at least, as of nuisance value only. Although Hitler still had some lethal shots left in his locker—the "little blitz" on London in early 1944, and the "doodlebugs" and rockets that prolonged Britain's ordeal until the launching sites were smashed—from that time on, German factories were trundling out fighters, not bombers, and that was no way to win a war. There can be no doubt that the enemy was forced into this defensive posture by the USAAF's daylight raids.

For the participants—the men who flew the airplanes—there were many differences between a day mission in a Fortress or a Liberator and a night operation in a British bomber. For one thing, the RAF crews tried not to tangle with the night fighters, and used various tactics—electronic countermeasures, spoof attacks, and feints—to put them off the scent. The fliers of the Eighth, on the other hand, deliberately set out to take the fighters on: with the great formations shining in the sunlight and leaving condensation trails for many miles behind them, they presented a challenge no defending air force could refuse. In this, the USAAF's air divisions could be likened to regiments of cavalry, riding high upon a hillside, silhouetted on the skyline, with guidons fluttering and bugles blowing the charge; "Butch" Harris's men, on the other hand, were more like the infantry, moving through the lines in darkness, with blackened faces and muffled tread.

It was when they reached their targets that the Allied fliers shared a mutual experience. There the reception was very much the same; it just looked rather different. The crewmen saw ahead of them an apparently impenetrable barrier of flak, standing in their way from the start of the bomb run to the release point and beyond. At night it appeared as a million sparks among the groping searchlights; by day, as a sky full of lumps of dirty cotton. That was what they had to fly through, day or night. There was no point in trying to dodge between the shell bursts: in evading one they might fly into another. Nor was there any chance of dodging, even if they wanted to, once the airplane was committed to the bomb run. From

The Avro Lancaster, above, was one of the best Allied bombers of the war. Entering service with RAF Bomber Command in 1942, the Lanc was the primary British heavy bomber of the RAF, RCAF, and Commonwealth squadrons. The type delivered more than 600,000 tons of bombs in 156,000 sorties, and carried various ordnance, from high-explosives, to incendiaries, and the massive 'blockbusters,' as well as the Barnes Wallis 'bouncing bomb' used in Operation Chastise, the attack on the great dams of the Ruhr valley in May 1943; left: The other very successful British heavy bomber of WW2 was the RAF's Handley-Page Halifax, a versatile aircraft of high achievement.

top left: Women war workers completing a Boeing B-17 Flying Fortress bomber in 1943; above: A B-17 tail gunner on a USAAF base in England during the Second World War; left: Factory-fresh B-17s at an American air depot in wartime England; right: The instrument panel, throttles and control yoke of a B-17 bomber.

that moment on, it was the man with his thumb on the bomb release button who was in control, and he had eyes only for the aiming point or the lead plane's bomb bay.

However similar the physical experiences over the target, there was a marked distinction in the human aspect. The crewmen of a USAAF bomber were flying close to guys they knew: at the controls of the Fortress above their starboard wing was the pilot's buddy; one of the navigator's poker school was flying in the nose of the airplane on their left; the gunners in the lead ship shared a billet with their own. When any of those aircraft lost a battle with a fighter, or a flak battery scored a lethal hit, there was a personal interest in seeing who got out. Everyone should, of course, be concentrating on his job, but when you knew that Ed

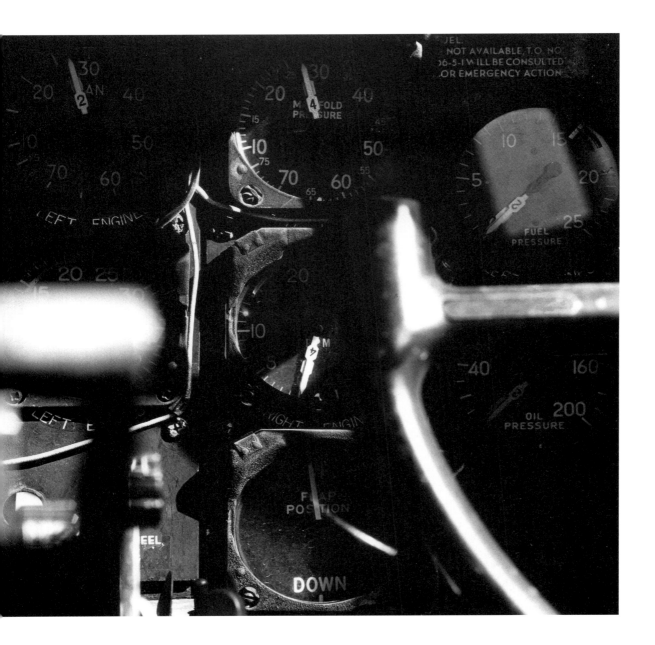

was in that ship, and little Virgil from Ohio, you couldn't help but watch and whisper, "Come on, you guys, get the hell out of there!" At night it was different, and utterly impersonal. No one could identify the men who had just disappeared in a blinding flash of light; no one had a clue who was trapped inside that burning Lancaster making a meteoric arc across the sky. The crew of a night bomber were seven men essentially alone.

There is no part of the eight thousand square miles of England known as East Anglia that stands over four hundred feet above the sea. This, and the fact that the land is agricultural, containing no more than a half-dozen towns of any size, made it eminently suitable for siting bomber airfields. Some had been constructed before the war began and, by the end of 1944,

top: Staff and personnel of Eighth Air Force Bomber Command, at High Wycombe in 1944; above: The shoulder patch worn by members of the Eighth in WW2; left: The flying goggles of an Eighth USAAF airman.

a total of ninety-eight RAF or USAAF, were operational. If you walked ten miles in any direction from, say, Rattlesden or Deopham Green, you would be within hailing distance of another bomber base.

Further north in Lincolnshire the scene was much the same. Twenty-five RAF bases lay between the coastline and the river Trent, and from 10,000 feet on a clear night over Lincoln, you could see the Drem lights of a dozen fields. Some were so close that their traffic patterns overlapped; at Scampton, for example, when a southwest wind prevailed, the pilots would fly a right-hand pattern, while their neighbours at Dunholme Lodge made their circuits to the left. For both bomber forces, climbing to altitude, whether in darkness or in cloud by day, was a hazardous procedure, and midair collisions inevitably occurred. Every British pilot breathed a sigh of relief when he turned on his first course, every American when he emerged into the clear.

In press releases, the RAF seldom publicized the altitudes at which its bombers flew. The USAAF, with no cause for secrecy, revealed that the Fortresses could operate at 30,000 feet. The information intrigued the British public: how did the crews survive at such a height? Perhaps, it was argued, the well-established fact that Americans were fed from early childhood on T-bone steaks and pumpkin pie contributed to their extraordinary stamina. In the interests of medical research, an English doctor accompanied a Fortress crew on a training exercise. That he became unconscious halfway through the flight merely reinforced the theory that the Yanks were supermen.

The Eighth's combat formations were planned with two main purposes in mind: one, to maximize the firepower of the bomber's guns, and two, to concentrate the bombing pattern on the MPI while ensuring that no bombs hit another aircraft as they fell. These were considerations that had little application to the RAF's night bombers, in which the crews found their own way to the target, fought individual battles with the fighters (but only if they had to), and made the bomb runs on their own. The operations staff at High Wycombe did their best to limit "friendly" damage by splitting the attacks into waves, each lasting ten or fifteen minutes, but the inevitable navigation errors meant that some Halifaxes and Stirlings infringed the timing of the higher-flying Lancasters, and vice versa. Many British aircraft were found, on return, to have been damaged by bombs from aircraft flying above them, and no one will ever know how many more went down. Aiming point photographs, brought home by Lancasters, often showed the black silhouettes of four-engined aircraft that had flown into the cross wires as the bombs began to fall.

Although the organization and structure of command in the USAAF and the RAF were basically similar, there were certain differences in style and designations. Commissioned officers in the U.S. Army Air Force naturally held military ranks, while the RAF, on gaining the status of an independent service toward the end of the First World War, had adopted new ones of its own. In ascending order, an American second lieutenant ranked with a British pilot officer, a first lieutenant with a flying officer, a captain with a flight lieutenant, a major with a squadron leader, a lieutenant colonel with a wing commander, a colonel with a group captain, a brigadier general with an air commodore and so on.

The basic combat unit in both forces was the squadron, and one or two RAF bomber squadrons occupied a "station"; a number of stations were controlled by group HQ, some-

The pilot of this Eighth Air Force bomber crew giving last minute instructions to his gunners prior to their pre-dawn takeoff on a bombing mission to a German target.

times with a "base station" as an intermediary, and the group staffs answered to the commander in chief at High Wycombe. Although the RAF fighter squadrons might form wings for combat purposes, in the bomber force the wing was no longer an operational formation. In the Eighth Air Force, groups of four squadrons occupied a "base," fifteen groups comprised a bombardment wing (later to be known as an air division), which responded to the commanding general, Eighth Bomber Command Headquarters at Daws Hill.

The problem of nomenclature occasioned by the fact that "groups" and "wings" meant different things to the USAAF and the RAF, and that the RAF did not recognize an "air division," were compounded by the anomalies of rank. In the prewar RAF, these had born some relation to the holder's duties: pilot officers were pilots, flying officers flew airplanes, flight lieutenants led flights, and squadron leaders led squadrons. The war had brought upgradings: the command of main force flights and squadrons rated one rank more, and two more in No. 8 Group, the Pathfinder Force. The USAAF, on the other hand, saw no need to escalate its gradings. The American commander of a Fortress squadron, visiting his equivalent on a British pathfinder base, might have been surprised to find himself heavily outranked. It may have been as well for interservice harmony that these visits were infrequent: squadron commanders, RAF or USAAF, had little time for making social calls.

below: On the control tower at Shipdham; right: Wake-up call for this American airman.

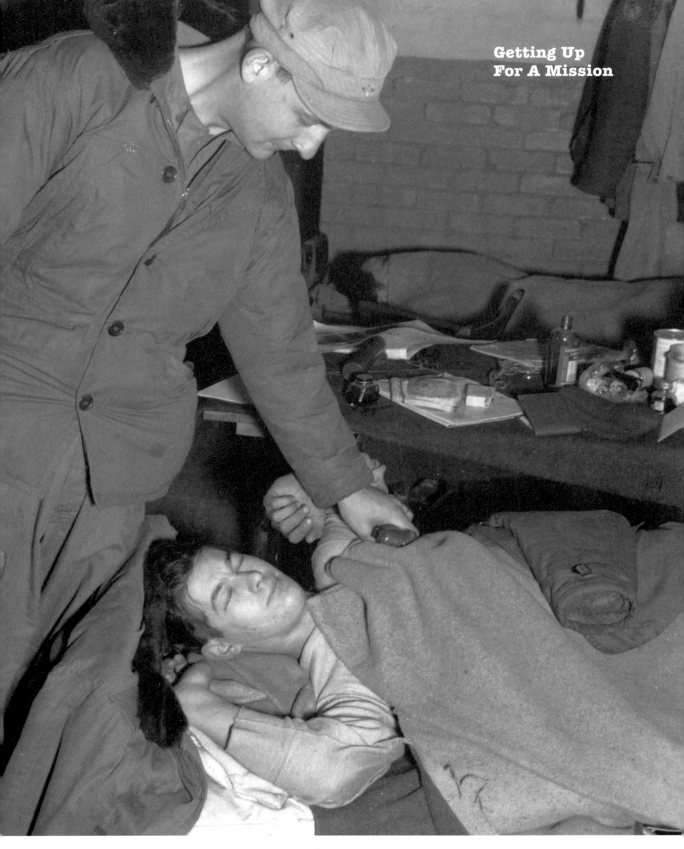

Everyone at some time has awakened in the morning knowing that a big day lies ahead. It might be a crucial business meeting, an opening night on stage, your first match with the "A" team, a university examination. You know it has to happen, and in a way you're glad of it; in another way you dread it, and you wish it were tomorrow, not today. All bomber crewmen experienced such feelings, and with some intensity. They woke to many big days, and knew that any one might be their last on earth.

The start of one such big day for a combat flier was described by ball turret gunner Ken Stone of the 381st Bomb Group: "The night officer came around every barracks and woke us up. As a gunner, you had no prior notification. If a mission was called, they just came and woke you up. If they said to hurry, we usually didn't shave. That kind of irritated when you had your oxygen mask on, but I didn't have much of a beard then, anyway. They gave us time to have breakfast. I'd have eggs—real eggs—fried or scrambled, and lots of Spam. I swore I'd never eat Spam again. But it was regular food, the same as the officers ate."

The reveille routine at Debach in the time of Larry Bird, who flew twenty-three missions with the 493rd Bomb Group, was rather better organized. "You'd go to the bulletin board at five or six o'clock in the afternoon to check which crews were flying the next day. If you were down to fly, you'd try and get to bed a little earlier than usual."

Paul Sink, the rear gunner in Bird's crew, took that sequence further: "After breakfast, we went to the main briefing. The room was dimly lit like a theater, with huge maps on the wall. A jagged line showed the courses, the initial point, the bomb run, and the rally point. It showed where you would pick up the fighter cover, where you would lose it, and where you would pick it up again."

"After the main briefing, Bird continued, "the pilots, navigators and bombardiers had individual briefings, while the rest of the crew collected their guns from the armament shack. We went out to the hardstands, got the props pulled through and the guns installed, and gave the airplane a complete preflight check—intercom and oxygen systems and everything. By then it was usually getting to be almost daylight. Sometimes the moon would still be visible. The pilots got the engines ticking over, and we'd all move out and go down the taxi strip in a long line. Then we'd wait our turn to take off. It would be getting lighter all the time."

Charles J. Bosshardt, who flew twenty missions in a B-24 of the 458th Bomb Group, recalled one of those navigator's briefings at Horsham St Faith in February 1945: "That morning they got us up at three-thirty and we were briefed for the marshaling yard at Rheine. We navigators were always in there at briefing long after the rest of the crews had gone out to the aircraft, and I was usually in a sweat when I joined them. This time, I was the last one out. I piled my equipment into a truck and set out to find the plane. We drove out past all the 753rd Squadron revetments but I couldn't spot it. I had the driver turn around. I jumped out and checked a few that looked like U141 but none of them was it. In desperation I asked another pilot to check his flimsy for the revetment number. He told me that my plane was not in this revetment. I was getting worried by then because it was just a few minutes until stations time. Finally I started checking the marshalled ships. The first few were from another squadron, then came our squadron. The third one up was U141. I ran up and got our nose gunner to go back to the truck with me and help carry my junk. We trotted back and got it and started weaving our way through the prop blades. Just as I dumped my stuff in the nose the pilot started warming the engines. I dragged my body up on the flight deck and waited

Pre-mission routine on an 8USAAF base
in WW2England; above: Breakfast; below:
Mission briefing for fighter escort pilots;
right: A B-17 gunner dressing for the flight..

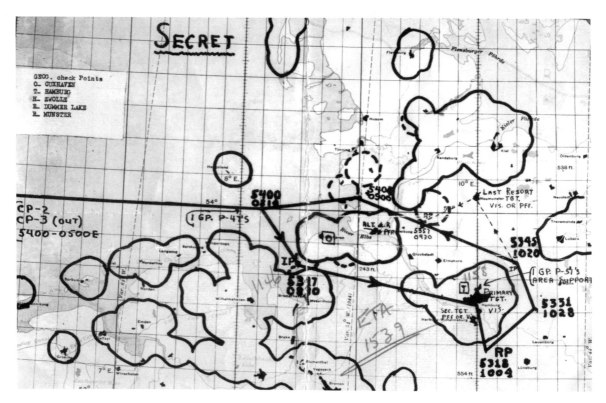

at top: An 8AF mission map showing
flak concentrations; above: Time hack;
right: Gunner leaving on a mission.

left: Preparing a bomb on this B-24 Liberator hardstand in England, for delivery to a German target; below: An Eighth Air Force B-17 bomber crew member wearing an A2 leather flying jacket decorated with the name of his aircraft.

for takeoff. I was soaked in perspiration."

"As a lead crew," said radar operator Sidney Rapoport of the 94th Bomb Group, "we knew about the mission before the other crews and we were woken earlier. That was an interesting experience, getting up at two in the morning in a black winter night in East Anglia. It was icy outside when you went to the latrine. It was important to shave, and looking in the mirror, I always used to think: 'Mirror, mirror, is this the last time I'm going to look into you?' "

The RAF crews' preparation for a night operation varied little from station to station. Jack Clift of 463 Squadron described the beginning of a normal day. "I would go down to the flight engineers' office, the pilots to theirs, the navigators to theirs, and so on. The section leaders would tell us if there was anything new we ought to know about. By lunchtime, we'd have found out if ops were on, and later they'd put the battle order up showing which crews were scheduled. If we were on the list, we'd take the aircraft for a test flight, just to make sure everything was okay. About tea time you'd know what the petrol load was, and that would give you some idea about the trip. If it was 2,154 gallons—maximum petrol—you knew it was a long one. Most of ours were 2154s. There would be separate briefings for us and the other crew members, and then the main briefing, with the CO and the wing commander. When you walked in, you looked at the big map on the wall and the red ribbon zigzagging out to the target—we never went straight there—and you would say, 'Bloody hell, another snorter.' "

Although RAF briefings usually took place some twelve hours after the USAAF's, they were very similar in content and in sequence. They would include a description of the target and its strategic significance, the intended tactics, the system of control, the heights and courses to be flown, the expected opposition, the assigned supporting forces, and a weather forecast. There would be a time check for the navigators and some words of exhortation from the colonel or group captain in command. On a USAAF base, at this point, it was not uncommon for the chaplain to offer a short prayer. RAF crews were given no such overt benison before they took to the air, nor would the padre normally be present; he was available, however, for those who sought his blessing, and would probably be waiting when the crews returned, dispensing mugs of cocoa and a warm word of greeting before they were debriefed.

'After the briefing," Jack Clift continued, "there'd be a meal, a nice meal of bacon and eggs, and then you'd relax, lie down on your bed and have a rest for half an hour. Of course, you'd keep thinking about what you were going to be doing for the next ten hours or so. And then, down to the crew room, pick up the parachutes, get dressed in your gear, into the crew bus, out to the flights, into the aircraft, and away."

Clift had the advantage of being based at Waddington, a compact, prewar station; facilities on other airfields were more widely spread out. Once an airman left his billet in the morning, he had left it for the day, as Reg Payne of 50 Squadron remembered of his time at Skellingthorpe. "If there was a break between the flying meal and takeoff, we never went back to the billet, because it was a mile and a half away from the mess, and the mess was a mile from the operations room. We just used to sit down somewhere and close our eyes for a while."

Briefings at Skellingthorpe, as Payne recalled them, demanded more than average attention. "The CO was very strict. He'd brief you on what time start-up and takeoff were, what time the first wave set off, the course, the engine revs and boost, the height you had to be at the first turning point, what colors the markers were . . . and then he would call someone out—any crew member—and make him repeat it in front of everybody. If you made a cock-up of it, and he thought you hadn't been listening, you were struck off the raid, and a substitute would fly in your place. That was considered a black mark for the crew. I was a wireless op, and a lot of it didn't mean much to me, but I used to memorize it all."

The body clock of the average young man tells him to be active in the daytime and to sleep at night; it does not readily accept a different regime. To help the night bomber men in staying alert throughout their missions, the medicos supplied caffeine-based stimulants known as "wakey-wakey" pills. "We'd never take them," said Payne, "until the aircraft was rumbling down the runway, because we'd had many occasions when the raid was scrubbed at the last minute and we'd be up the creek—awake all night for nothing."

Pre-dawn on the hardstand of an Eighth Air Force B-17 bomber as the crew and ground personnel are going through the engine start-up procedure.

A fine study of a last minute engine adjustment before the day's mission.

Key Targets

When Franklin Delano Roosevelt, Winston Churchill, and Joseph Stalin conferred at Casablanca in January 1943, the fate of two commands—Eaker's and Harris's—rested in their hands. If they accepted Stalin's demand for a second front in Europe (and Roosevelt was sympathetic to the Russian argument), Overlord would be mounted, and the strategic air offensive would be finished before it had properly begun. General Eisenhower would take charge as the Supreme Commander Allied Forces Europe, and the bombers would be total-ly committed to ground-support operations. It would thus be good-bye to the bomber chiefs' dream of reducing Germany's morale and matériel to the point where the Allied armies would merely be required as an occupation force.

Even if the British view prevailed—that the Overlord invasion should wait upon Husky (an advance into Europe through Sicily and Italy)—the bomber commanders still had problems in their own backyards. The admirals, both in Washington and London, were propounding that the airplanes under construction for the Eighth Air Force should go to the Pacific, that Harris's bombers should concentrate on U-boats, and that the H2S radars his navigators sorely needed should instead be fitted in the anti-submarine patrol planes of Coastal Command.

Another, if lesser, problem was that not everyone in Britain supported Harris's campaign. Quoting the devastation of Essen and Cologne as instances, a prominent churchman was leading a number of gentle souls in protesting against what they saw as a slaughter of the innocent, and two respected, albeit armchair, strategists were complaining that an undue proportion of the British national war effort was being absorbed by Harris's command. The great majority, however, of the British people remained solidly in favor of the bomber offensive. Most seemed to understand that Queensberry rules and padded gloves were out when you were fighting for your life. Harris's aircrews stood high in the public's affection and esteem, perhaps not quite so high as the fighter pilots had while the Battle of Britain was being fought above their homes, but high enough to ensure the bomber boys a welcome when they spent an evening in the "local" or a leave in town.

As things turned out, Winston Churchill was well satisfied with the outcome of the summit conference. However readily he had welcomed Russia as an ally, he was not altogether displeased that the Wehrmacht and the Red Army should have another year in which to grind each other down. Eaker and Harris too, both came out of Casablanca pretty well. The essence of the Moroccan deliberations, as distilled and decanted by the planning staffs, eventually reached the bomber chiefs as the Pointblank directive. "Your primary aim," it began, "will be the progressive destruction and dislocation of the German military, industrial and economic system, and the undermining of the morale of the German people to a point where their capacity for armed resistance is fatally weakened."

It says much for Eaker's staff work and his powers of persuasion that, although none of his bombers had yet flown over Germany and half his sorties had failed to reach their targets, his imprint was heavy on what followed in the document. Far from requiring him to renounce daylight bombing and join the night offensive, as the British had suggested, the directive authorized continued day attacks "to destroy objectives unsuitable for night bombing, to impose heavy losses on the German day fighter force, and to contain its strength away from the Russian and Mediterranean theaters."

There was a sop for the admirals in that the first objectives on the Pointblank list were U-boat facilities; airfields and airplane factories came next; and then, in order, ball-bearing plants, oil refineries, synthetic rubber works, and transportation targets. It also transpired that an Eaker reference to bombing "round the clock" had found favor with the British prime minister, who had rolled the phrase around his tongue in Morocco and used it ever after as his own.

None of this was any skin off Harris's nose. "When precision targets are bombed by the Eighth Air Force in daylight," he read with satisfaction in the follow-up to the directive, "the

below: A Rhine bridge destroyed in a USAAF attack on Koblenz; right: A Halifax crew returns from a night raid; bottom left: Target markers during an RAF raid; bottom right: Flak damage to an RAF Lancaster bomber.

effort should be completed and complemented by RAF attacks against the surrounding industrial area at night." "This," he later wrote, "gave me a very wide range of choice and allowed me to attack pretty well any German industrial city of 100,000 inhabitants and above." So, for the citizens of Essen and Cologne, Pointblank meant that the worst was yet to come; for the people of Hamburg, Frankfurt, Stuttgart, Mannheim, and points east, that the bombers would get to them in turn; for the Berliners, that the time was not far off when they would be subjected to the greatest air onslaught ever to be mounted on a European city.

Very few RAF men had any doubt that they were doing what they had to do. For them, the problem wasn't one of ethics but of method—of technique. Many of the pilots, trained to high standards in formation flying, regretted they never had the chance to use that skill; when they watched the air armadas of the Eighth go forth to war, there was a certain envy in their gaze; the bomb-aimers, too, often wished that they were equipped with the USAAF's

33

top left: The breached Möhne dam after Operation Chastise in May 1943; left: A heavy saturation attack by RAF Lancasters; above: RAF bomber aircrewmen awaiting transportation out to their Lancasters, in a photo believed to be of No. 9 Squadron personnel at RAF Bardney, Lincolnshire.

apparatus—the computerized, gyrostabilized Norden Mark XV bombsight—with which, claimed the bombardiers (after a drink or two) they could drop a five-hundred-pounder into a pickle barrel from 25,000 feet; many an air gunner would have willingly exchanged all his .303 machine-guns for one American .50-caliber.

One major problem the bomber forces shared was the European weather. At an early meeting, Harris had warned Eaker (perhaps with some exaggeration) that on four days out of five his bombardiers would never see the ground. "So we'll bring the bombs home and try another day," had been the American's reply, but as time went on, Eaker realized that his crews were flying too many noneffective missions. In cloudy conditions Eaker and General Frederick Anderson (the Eighth's bomber chief) were obliged to turn, as Harris had before them, to the magic eye of radar ("Mickey" to the Eighth), aided when required by target-marking pyrotechnics. This was a method to which the RAF was well accustomed, and for the purposes of saturation bombing it was adequate. For precision bombing it was not, but that had to be accepted. The round-the-clock policy required sustained attack, and in much of Europe's winter (and often in summer) you either bombed through cloud or not at all.

To achieve concentration or accuracy using ground target markers was difficult enough; using sky markers over thick cloud cover, it was practically impossible. Then, the parachuted flares marked a point in the sky through which the bombs should fall. Theoretically, if the aircraft's speed and heading were both exactly right, they should go on to hit the target: realistically, they could miss it by many a mile. Certainly, the results could not compare with those to be achieved by the human eyeball looking down through a bombsight—and especially through the Norden.

It was only on the nights when the sky was clear and moonlit, or at times when a feature of the target—a river or a coastline—showed up clearly in the light of flares and fires, that the RAF crews made the sort of bomb runs for which they had been trained. For the most part they depended on the target-marking efforts of No. 8 Group, the specially selected elite Pathfinder Force flying Lancasters, Halifaxes, and Mosquitoes, using the latest types of radar, and led by the brilliant, if independently minded, Australian Air Vice Marshal D.C.T. Bennett.

"Donald Bennett," said Lancaster pilot Alan Foreman, "was a highly qualified man, and he would tolerate no backsliding at all. None whatsoever. He often came around the squadrons and complained about creepback. What happened was, a bomb-aimer would be keen to get rid of his bombs and he'd bomb a little short of the aiming point.

above and below: Short Stirlings of RAF Bomber Command; bottom left: The Lancaster *Able Mabel*, a veteran of ninety-five bombing raids.

top left: RAF airmen cycling on their base in 1942; above: A Lancaster about to touch down after a trip to Germany; far left: The cew of an RAF Lancaster; left: RAF sergeants in their mess.

The big, lumbering Stirling lacked the performance of either the Lancaster or the Halifax. Sadly, not a single example of the Stirling remains.

The next aircraft would be shorter, and so on, shorter and shorter. Creepback. That's why the PFF was formed. They kept remarking the actual aiming point. They used colored markers, and the Germans got on to this. They used markers on the ground to distract the bombers. The PFF had to keep changing the colors. The "master bomber" would say, 'Bomb on the greens. Ignore the yellows in the northeast corner.' "

Keith Newhouse, who had flown his B-24, *Wallowing Wilbur*, from Florida, via Trinidad, Brazil, and French Morocco to join the Eighth Air Force, was to fly thirty-three missions with the 467th Bomb Group, and to earn the DFC and Air Medal with three clusters. He made this diary note a few days after his arrival at Rackheath airfield in Norfolk. "Wednesday, March 22, 1944. I spent an hour or two in our war room. All the dope the Eighth has on prospec-

tive targets is consolidated there for the study of combat crew officers. Maps, photographs, and pertinent data. Heavy flak concentrations are marked clearly, and anything that will help to identify the targets is brought to one's attention."

On the big daylight missions, however, target identification was not a matter of concern for the majority of pilots. Their task was to keep station on the leaders of their squadrons who, in turn, were maintaining their positions in the group formation. That was never an easy operation, riding the slipstream and the heavy condensation trails. The contrails, as Newhouse found, "made lovely photographs but were like clouds to a pilot flying formation. When we were flying close for mutual firepower, they were dense. Ducking in and out of them added to the terror of crashing into a friend." Except for certain special targets, the Lancasters' bombed at around 20,000 feet, somewhat lower for the Halifaxes and lower still for the Stirlings and Wellingtons. The B-24 formations of the Eighth sought to make their bomb run heights between 20,000 and 23,000 feet, while the B-17s generally occupied the height-band from 24,000 to 27,000. Occasionally the weather required them to climb higher, as Paul Sink recalled: ""It was when we went to Bittefeld on March 17, 1945. At 30,000 feet we were just above the cloud. All the guns on the airplane were frozen solid, and the German fighters had the same problem. The strangest thing was that I saw a parachute floating down from above us, on the left side of our airplane. The temperature then was probably sixty degrees below, and there was this parachute with a person hanging from it."

Throughout the latter part of the air offensive, the enemy oil industry always had a high priority on the USAAF's target list, but it seldom featured on the RAF's. This was understandable: apart from the fact that Arthur Harris was suspicious of what he called "panacea" targets, oil installations, with their compact layout, were not entirely suitable for area attack. In June 1944, when four attacks were made on oil plants in the Ruhr, the results were disappointing and the losses were severe. Some eight hundred sorties cost over ninety aircraft. An attack three months later, on Sterkrade and Bottrop, was no more successful: only twenty-five bomb-aimers out of nearly three hundred claimed to have found the target through the cloud; the rest dropped their loads on "the estimated positions of other Ruhr cities."

That operation stayed in the memory of Fred Allen, rear gunner of Halifax *Friday The Thirteenth*, based at Lissett near the Yorkshire coast, for an instance of what he described as "finger trouble." "The first time round," said Allen, "the bomb-aimer forgot to fuse the bombs. Next attempt, he didn't open the bomb doors. When you didn't bomb, you had to turn to port and go around again. Everybody else was turning starboard. The Jerries weren't much concerned with the ones that had bombed, but they were with those that hadn't. It got a bit hot. The skipper said, 'If you don't drop the buggers this time, I will'—meaning he'd use the jettison bar. We dropped them, all right."

"We'd generally have three targets," said Lawrence Drew, who flew a B-17 with the 384th Bomb Group throughout the last five months of the war. "A primary, a secondary, and a tertiary. Well, a lot of times the leader couldn't hit the primary, so he'd go on to the secondary, then if you couldn't hit any of the three, we'd have some targets of opportunity. You'd search around for anywhere you thought would do some good. You couldn't hang around too long because you'd be back too late and get into a conflict with the timing of the RAF."

left: Target folders at Eighth Air Force Bomber Command headquarters, High Wycombe, in the Second World War; right: The refueling process on the hardstand of a B-17 in England.

On the bomber stations of the Eighth, the ground crews have filled the gas tanks overnight, checked the engines, and serviced all the systems. The armorers are still winching five-hundred-pounders into the bomb bay when the first crewmen arrive in the early morning hours. The gunners install their weapons in the turrets, the radio operator tests the RT and the intercom, and the top gunner, doubling as engineer, checks the oxygen supply and generally prepares the airplane for flight. The next truck to come by brings the pilots, the navigator (if not delayed at briefing), and the bombardier. Soon, the airfield and all the countryside around right: The waist gunners' area in the fuselage of a Boeing B-17 Flying Fortress bomber. Visible are the left and right-mounted Browning .50 calibre machine-guns, ammunition boxes and, in the distance, the upper portion of the ball turret structure; below: A 1943 guide for U.S. Army Air Force gunners, prepared by the Operations Analysis Section and the AAF Training Aids Division.

it echo with the roar of two hundred Wright R-1820 engines, 1,200 horsepower each, warming up for flight. On a signal from the tower, the airplanes roll out of the hardstands and, in sequence according to the traffic plan, twist and turn along the perimeter track to the checkered trailer beside the takeoff point.

With the engines idling and the airplanes trembling like greyhounds in the slips, the lead pilots wait for a green light from the tower. Tense at their stations, the crewmen cannot help but think of what the next few hours will bring. Too late now to wish you'd gone on sick call, too late now to wish you hadn't joined the Air Force; this is why they gave you the rank and silver wings.

The Aldis lamp shines green; the first airplane in line moves forward and swings onto the runway, heading into the wind. Holding the brakes on, the pilot guns the engines one last time. A group of well-wishers, gathered by the trailer, wave and wish the crew a safe return. Slowly gaining pace, the big bomber makes its run. At the moment when the airspeed needle comes around to takeoff speed, if the pilot's instinct tells him that the plane will fly, he gently pulls the yoke back and the mission has begun . . .

For the night bombers' takeoffs, it was much the same procedure, although movements on the airfield, usually in darkness, were necessarily laborious and slow. Circumnavigation of the long perimeter track, marked by the dim, blue glim-lamps, widely spaced, called for careful use of outboard engines in conjunction with the rudders and the brakes (unlike USAAF bombers' braking systems, those in British heavies were not differential). The bomb-aimer could help by shining an Aldis lamp on the near side of the taxiway, but every pilot knew that one wheel off the tarmac, sinking in the mud, could bring the whole squadron to a halt. Arriving safely at the caravan/trailer, he still had the problem of steering down the runway with no centerline to see. Once airborne, however, all he had to do was to keep on climbing as high as he could go, avoiding other aircraft—also climbing in their hundreds—on the way.

For the Eighth Air Force pilot, at this point in the mission, the hardest part had yet to come: he had to find the lead plane of his squadron and take his station in the combat box formation. "One time when we were assembling," Charles Bosshardt remembered, "it was still so dark you could hardly see the other ships. There were ships everywhere going in all directions. The pilot had the tail gunner flashing the Aldis lamp from his position, and the top gunner had the trouble light on making himself a lighthouse. The sunrise was beautiful. There was a narrow band of flaming red between the black sea and the clouds. And as it gradually grew lighter the clouds rolled in lower and lower and finally the mission was called off."

"You had to rally with all the other groups," said Larry Bird. "The wing would assemble, and then another wing, and finally after about an hour of this you would be ready to start moving in one big stream. You were on your way across the water, and by the time you reached Holland it was daylight. You could see this long strip of sand. And clouds, always clouds everywhere."

Road and rail communications were the targets for the bombers in mid-April 1944; on Easter Monday, 166 Squadron' Lancasters lined up on the long runway at Kirmington in Lincolnshire for an attack on the railway yards at Aulnoye. Four aircraft took off safely but the fifth swung off the runway, the pilot overcorrected, and the wheels collapsed. The instant detonation of nine tons of high explosive made a crater fifty feet in diameter and fifteen in

view of the cockpit of
Boeing B-17 bomber.

depth. Pieces of the Lancaster flew in all directions, and a watching officer reported that a Merlin engine had missed his head by inches. By six o'clock next morning, the runway was repaired and, that evening, the squadron joined an attack on Aachen.

As the Eighth Air Force multiplied, putting more and more bombers in the air on every mission, the pilots often had difficulty in finding their lead planes, especially when the visibility was poor. The lead crews fired signal cartridges of prearranged colors over the assembly points, but as Colonel Dale O. Smith of the 384th Bomb Group observed: "When you look

below: B-17s of the 390th Bomb Group, Eighth Air Force, waiting their turn to take off on a bombing mission; A night view of a Lancaster running up her engines before take-off.

for the leader he isn't firing flares, and when someone in your plane sees them, by the time he calls you, the flares are out and all you see is two trails of smoke where the leader was a few minutes ago.''

Dale Smith's answer was to have his lead crews fire a constant stream of flares, and to keep on firing them until the squadrons formed. Another solution adopted by the Eighth was to deploy brightly-painted airplanes—usually the war-weary B-17s or B-24s—which, having served as airborne assembly points, returned to their bases when the wings had formed.

Assembling the airplanes into elements of three, the elements into squadrons, the squadrons into groups, and the groups into wings, called for careful timing and precision flying. By the time Ira Eaker's vision of bombing round the clock had become a reality, the Eighth had devised a method which, however laborious it may seem to us now, had the advantage that it worked. On one mission, for example, the targets were railroad yards and tank plants in Berlin. Over East Anglia, the base of the cloud was at 3,000 feet and the tops were at 6,000. On forty Eighth Air Force bases, the takeoffs began at 7.00 a.m., and the bombers followed one another into the air at sixty-second intervals. Then each pilot headed for the Buncher—his group radio beacon—some twelve miles away, made a full turn around it, and flew a climbing racetrack pattern between the Buncher and the Splasher base beacon, until he reached clear air.

Once above the cloud tops, flying in wide circles around the Bunchers, the squadrons

took their places in the group formations and, at 8.15, the group lead pilots turned out of their orbits and headed for the wing assembly points, flying dogleg courses that could be shortened or extended to allow the other group formations to fit in. From the wing assembly points, still on dogleg courses, the bombers converged to form divisions above the Norfolk coast. Almost two hours to the minute since the first takeoffs began, the people of Cromer heard the muffled thunder as 450 B-17s of the 1st Air Division passed above their town. A few miles to the south, 350 B-24s of the 2nd Air Division roared across Great Yarmouth while, over Southwold on the Suffolk coast, 530 of the 3rd Air Division's B-17s turned to join the great armada heading for "Big B." It didn't always work out quite like that. "Our first combat mission was a sort of farce," revealed Bill Ganz of the 398th Bomb Group. "There was heavy overcast and we had trouble forming in the group. Eventually we picked up a group that was headed east and tagged along." W.W. Ford of the 92nd had a similar experience: "We made two orbits of the beacon and we weren't picking anybody up. We'd been briefed to go on after a certain time if that happened, but when we broke out of the cloud around 22,000 feet there wasn't another airplane anywhere in sight. Over the coast of France we picked up a lead plane from our group and formed up on him. In the next twenty minutes we picked up a B-24 from the 2nd Air Division and three more B-17s from all over. We went on to Munich with this bunch, made the bomb run, and came back in formation. As soon as we hit the English coast everybody said, 'Good-bye, nice flying with you.' "

Views of the de Havilland Mosquito manufacturing process, including an aerial photo of de Havilland's Canadian Mosquito assembly plant. Much of the work on the Mosquito was done by furniture and other wood-working factories and relatively few highly skilled craftsmen were required in the preparation, construction and assembly of the wooden aircraft. The D.H. 98 Mosquito, in its basic fighter version, was armed with four 20mm cannon and four .303 machine-guns. The bomber version could carry up to 2,000 pounds of bombs.

The Mosquito was certainly one of the finest aircraft to bring the daylight war to Germany. It was fully capable of making long-range attacks without fighter escort and was considered by the Germans to be one of the greatest Allied aerial threats, prior to the appearance in German skies of the North American P-51 Mustang fighter early in 1944. The Mosquito was one of the fastest and most versatile propeller-driven aircraft in history.

British and American air bases in World War Two England were big and sprawling affairs, with considerable distances to be covered by the residents. The bicycle proved to be an efficient transport for many; top: American Red Cross girls served coffee and doughnuts to airmen on the many English bases during the war; above: Fliers cooking eggs to their liking on a rare day when real eggs were provided—as opposed to powdered eggs, the standard fare of the time, which could, according to many airmen, "gag a buzzard."

right: The routine mission-day ritual of sweating 'em in after the raid. Officers tended to crowd the balcony rail of the control tower when the planes of the group were reported to be approaching the field; below: First Lieutenant Ray Wild and the crew of *Mizpah*, one of eight B-17s Wild flew during his tour of duty at Podington in Bedordshire in 1943-44.

Most Eighth Air Force men were given a week or two to get accustomed to life on an English airfield before they were committed to the fight. 1st Lt. Ray Wild, who arrived at Podington, Bedfordshire, to join the 92nd Bomb Group in September 1943, remembered his induction: "What they did when you showed up at the field, they had you shoot some landings, they checked out your crew, and they assigned you to a squadron. I ended up with the 325th. They had a wall with names on it—twelve missions, fourteen missions—and MIA, KIA. None of us knew what that meant. They showed you that and then they took you to the ready room, and you took your crew out flying formation for a short period of time, according to how fast they needed replacement crews to fly missions."

During this period of orientation, while they were flying cross-countries, learning to use the gee-box, dropping practice bombs, attending classroom studies (and learning that the letters on the wall meant "missing in action" and "killed in action"), the rule in some groups was that new arrivals were restricted to the base. "I was paid today in one-pound notes," Keith Newhouse noted at Rackheath, "I have a roll to choke a horse with and can do nothing with it. Can't buy a thing but a week's rations at the PX. We sit here and grow restless. We've been confined too long."

Ray Wild had won his wings at Moody Field, Valdosta, Georgia—"Mother Moody's Rest Camp" as it was sometimes known. Officially, Wild should not have been a pilot: on enlistment he was just six months too old. But he lied a little, made a careful alteration to his birth certificate, and for all the Air Force knew, he was eighteen months inside the limit. The things he remembered best about his time at Podington were all evoked by odors. "The first time it hit me was in that ready room. It was damp, musty—it had probably been that way for months. Then when you went into the briefing hut, you would always smell shaving lotion on those guys. It bothered the hell out of me. You had these heavy boots, heavy pants and jackets, and you opened them up and there was body smell then—not really unpleasant, but not pleasant because it was connected with the raid.

"Then we might sit waiting in the airplane for thirty, forty minutes, and there was a heavy smell of gasoline, but there was a ready room smell in their too, every time. I guess it was the odor of fear. On the runway, and for the first thousand feet or so, there'd still be the gasoline, and the smell of burnt cordite from the Channel on, after the gunners tested their guns. Coming back, we'd take off the oxygen mask and smoke a cigarette, and there was that smell, and always the cold sweat smell, until we got back on the ground. But after we landed, there was no gasoline smell, no cordite, no sweat—nothing that wasn't nice. It was all connected with fear and non-fear, I guess."

By the time W.W. Ford arrived at Podington in February 1945, Wild had not only completed his tour of missions with the 92nd, but had also undertaken another kind of tour: selling War Loan bonds in the States with Bing Crosby and Bob Hope. At Podington, the air war still went on. Three days after joining the 92nd, Ford's crew attended a dummy briefing session in the operations room. "It was fairly late when we finished, and we were about to be dismissed when the planes on that day's mission started coming back. One had been hit pretty badly, and they pulled up in front of Operations because it was the closest place to the hospital. The copilot and the tail gunner had been wounded, and a piece of flak had come through the nose and taken most of the back of the bombardier's head off. They unloaded these guys right in front of us, and it was a gory mess. That was our introduction to the way

left: The young Princess Elizabeth visiting one of the bases of the Eighth Air Force in WW2 England and the crew of the B-17 *Rose of York*; below: American airmen frequently entertained local British children at parties on the USAAF bases; right: The ambiance of a wartime Nissen hut on an airfield somewhere in England.

Of all the air bases occupied by the Americans in WW2 England, only a few were of the brick-built permanent variety, affording a relative bit of comfort to the lucky ones so assigned.

56

it was in combat." "We would make runs in formation," said Lawrence Drew, "on fictitious targets in England, get back to the base, and make some instrument approaches and landings for hours—just touch the wheels down, give it the gun, go around, and come back for another. All the time there was something to do—work on your radio operator's speed, your engineer's know-how—there was always training to do. We carried a very high fatigue factor at that time. If I had five minutes in a chow line I could go to sleep standing up."

The grind of training continued long after the preliminary phase; in fact, it never stopped. "When you weren't flying a mission," said Paul Sink, "you were flying a practice mission, or going to class, or something. You didn't have much spare time. That was for psychological rea-

sons: if you didn't have time to think, you didn't have time to get nervous, and if you didn't get nervous you were a better flier."

Part of the routine for the ground crew, and for many of the fliers not assigned to the mission, was to count the bombers coming home and watch them land. The top brass would assemble on the balcony of the control tower and sometimes on the roof. This was undoubtedly the best vantage point but not always the safest place to be. On March 17, 1945, the 493rd Bomb Group, having climbed above the cumulus to attack oil installations north of Leipzig, returned to find their airfield weathered in. "We were expecting a five-hundred-foot cloud base at Debach," said Paul Sink, "but it was a whole lot lower than that when we got

At the end of a raid, a belt of whisky and a quick bite usually awaited the returning fliers, along with an interrogation on their recent experience.

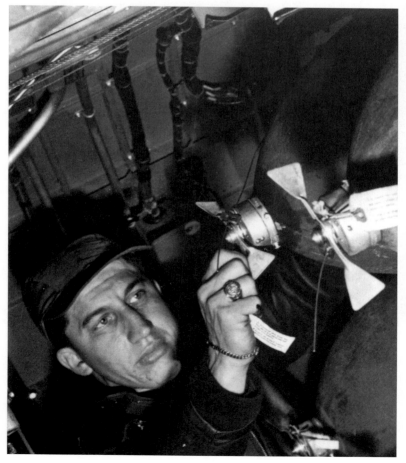

top left: Armorers bringing the bombs to the aircraft; left: An 8AF armorer checking the fuse of a bomb; above: The officers' club lounge on an 8AF base in England.

back. I heard the copilot say, 'I see the runway,' and we started letting down, but then the pilot said 'It's the goddamned control tower.' We cleared that thing by inches, and all of the people on it were jumping overboard." And, from 1941 onward, British airfields were never subjected to the sort of constant harassment inflicted on Luftwaffe bases by Mosquitoes and Marauders, but they were not immune from enemy intruders. Armorer Sam Burchell, whose

61

task at Seething was to load B-24 Liberators of the 448th Bomb Group with bullets and with bombs, remembered an attack in 1944. "They came in under the radar at the same time as the planes were coming home in the afternoon. They really did a job of strafing our base. Some people did get hurt and there were bombs going off and machine-guns and everything. That was the only time I saw what you might call combat. Of course, the air crews saw it every day."

Always, following a mission, there would be lots of questions in the operations block—interrogation, or debriefing, as it was later called. The airmen would be given something to relax them: cigarettes on the table, cocoa and a tot of rum for the RAF, coffee and perhaps a slug of scotch or brandy for the USAAF. The men who didn't care for alcohol would sometimes pass their ration to the ones who did. The crews, often weary and not always quite coherent, were questioned by officers of the Int/Ops branch.

"Did you hit the target?" the RAF men would be asked. "Was the marking good? Did you see the route markers? Were you attacked—where, and what action did you take? Did you see any aircraft go down, and where?" The USAAF crews were similarly quizzed. "Was the formation tight? Did you bomb the primary? Where did you encounter flak, where fighters? When this or that plane went down, how many chutes did you see?" Elsewhere in the operations block, there would be separate debriefings for the force commanders and lead pilots, navigators and bombardiers. From the answers to their questions, the debriefers would collate their raid reports and send them up the wire for analysis at wing or group HQ.

At most USAAF bases there was also a post-operational critique. The photographs of the target would be displayed and the group commander would make his observations. "Whenever they turned the lights out to show the strike photos," commented Charles Bosshardt of the 458th, "we would stretch out on the benches and nap. Our buddies would punch us to wake us up when the lights came on again. The critiques were a pain. We were all tired out and the colonel would be harping on about some failure to follow his instructions. I recall that he talked once about the loose formation. He said he could have flown his P-51 through it. One of the pilots spoke up and said, 'Well, hell, Colonel, I could have flown through too if I had a little plane like that.' "

Everyone quickly got accustomed to the sudden disappearance of roommates from the scene. "It was a bit upsetting sometimes," said Jack Clift. "You'd just get off to sleep and the RAF police would come in and go through their lockers, load all their gear into kit bags, take it out, and that's the last you'd see of them. They'd never be spoken of. We'd never talk about them after that."

left: An American air crew being driven to their waiting bomber; right: Dances on the station occasionally broke the routine. Here, a Yank and an English girl demonstrate the fine art of the Jitterbug.

Organized and headquartered at White Waltham, the ATA or Air Transport Auxiliary, was a civilian unit set up to ferry new, repaired, and damaged aircraft between UK factories and active squadrons. The American equivalent was the WASPs, or Women's Airforce Service Pilots.

65

left: Through extremely heavy flak over the
target, bombers of the 390th Bomb Group
fly a mission to Germany in 1944; top: B-24
Liberator air crew discuss the day's mission;
above: A personalized tail cone of a Flying
Fortress on an airfield in WW2 England.

On August 17, 1943, just one year to the day since Ira Eaker and his twelve B-17s flew the opening USAAF mission of the European air war, a force of thirty times that number—the largest yet assembled—made the first American deep-penetration sorties into the heart of Germany. In 1942, the objective had been barely forty miles across the Channel coast of France: the anniversary targets—the Messerschmitt factory in Regensburg and the ball-bearing plants in Schweinfurt—were both in Bavaria, and the route to the farthest passed over four hundred miles of hostile territory.

The attacks were planned to begin simultaneously—at ten minutes before 12.00 noon—with the aim of splitting the fighter opposition, but, as every fighting man knows, few plans survive exposure to the enemy, and in this case, the enemy was aided by the weather. The skies over Regensburg were reported to be clear, while Schweinfurt was obscured by ten-tenths cloud. To the RAF bomber crews, that would have mattered little: using radar marking, they would have rained the bombs down just the same. Not so the Eighth: at that stage of the war, Pinetree's edict was that bombardiers must see their targets.

On the Regensburg mission, 146 B-17s of the 4th Bomb Wing, flying in three combat box formations, were escorted by P-47s as far as the Belgian frontier. From there on, the bombers were subjected to a persistent onslaught by relays of fighters with cannon fire and rockets. The Luftwaffe mounted a formidable defense. Messerschmitt Me 109s, 110s and 210s, Focke-

Oscar Boesch, pilot of this Focke-Wulf Fw 190 fighter.

Wulf Fw 190s, and Junkers Ju 88s rose in their hundreds to repel the enemy bombers. In the Fortresses, the intercoms crackled with urgent admonitions: "Fire short bursts ... Don't waste rounds ... Lead 'em more." At times, it seemed to observers that the sky was filled with the debris of aerial combat: pieces of airplane, both American and German, life rafts and fuel tanks, exit doors and hatches. Some men fell with parachutes, other men without. Black smoke columns towered from burning bombers in the fields below.

After ninety minutes, the fighters broke away. Their controllers planned to reengage the bombers on their return. The B-17s swept on to Regensburg and, flying in the height band between 17,000 and 18,000 feet, released three hundred tons of bombs. The strike on the factory was well concentrated, and the results achieved by the 390th Bomb Group, in particular, of fifty-eight percent strikes within 1,000 feet of the aiming point and ninety-four percent inside 2,000 feet, were precision bombing of a high order.

Two months earlier, sixty Lancasters of No. 5 Group, having attacked a radar assembly plant on the north shore of Lake Constance, had continued on across the Alps and the Mediterranean Sea to land in Algeria. Three nights later, refueled and reloaded for the homeward flight, they had bombed the Italian naval base at La Spezia en route. That small force of Lancasters had flown the first shuttle mission of the war: the 4th Bomb Wing of the Eighth Air Force now embarked upon the second. Twenty-four aircraft had gone down; the survivors landed safely on airstrips in North Africa.

Three hours after the attack on Regensburg had ended, the 1st Bomb Wing's force of more than two hundred B-17s made their delayed approach on Schweinfurt, 120 miles to the northwest. Ken Stone, at twenty years of age, was manning the ball turret of the 381st Bomb Group's *Big Time Operator*. "I was awakened at three o'clock in the morning by the operations officer at Ridgewell, Captain Robert Nelson. I ate a hearty breakfast and rode out to the briefing room. Then I cleaned and dried my guns in the armament shack and installed them in the ball turret. I donned my flying clothes and sat down and waited until the officers came out at five-forty-five. Our plane was lead ship and our regular pilot, Lieutenant Lord, was flying as tail gunner to check the formation. Captain Briggs was flying as pilot and Major Hall as copilot. They started the engines at six o'clock and warmed them up. The control tower called and delayed takeoff one hour due to weather over the target. The engines were restarted at seven o'clock but before taxi time they delayed the mission again. I took a nap and the roar of the engines woke me up at nine o'clock. Then a red flare was fired from control and the mission was once more delayed. A truck came out with some Spam sandwiches. I managed to eat two of them ..."

Marvin T. Lord's crew had first become acquainted with the *Big Time Operator* at Pueblo, Colorado, while they were undergoing the final phase of their training. They had flown her to England, and on sixteen missions since they joined the 381st. Stone liked the airplane, and he liked his pilot; he particularly liked his pilot's name. "I'm flying with the Lord," he used to tell himself, "and the Lord will protect me."

Big Time Operator eventually took off at eleven-thirty. Stone entered the ball turret, and the group's twenty B-17s formed up over England with the rest of the wing. Again, the "little friends" gave cover to the limit of their range, but from Aachen onward the bombers flew alone. Refueled and rearmed, the German fighters were ready; so was Stone. "I watched them circle our group, sizing us up, and then they came in line abreast, with guns blazing. The

below: A Polish squadron Spitfire escorting bombers of the Deeethorpe-based 401st Bomb Group; Prime Minister Winston Churchill meeting with chief Spitfire test pilot Alex Henshaw at Castle Bromwich in 1944; below: Lancaster production.

first pass, they came head-on at us, and it was the first time they'd done this. It was something new to us, and very effective. Then they flew underneath our plane and into the formation. They were Me 109s and Fw 190s that were hitting us. I had plenty of good shots, but I don't know if I got any—I was too busy shooting at the next one coming in—but I'm sure I didn't waste all my ammunition. Lord said one blew up after it passed us, and he figured I might have gotten it. Two wing men were hit—Painter on our left and Jarvis on our right. The waist gunners waved to us and then they went down. Lieutenant Darrow's plane had an engine knocked out, but he managed to keep up with the formation. After what seemed like hours, the fighters disappeared.

"We were met," Stone went on, "by a medium amount of flak over the target. That was the scariest thing—when you had to go over the target and your bombardier controlled the plane. You had to fly steady, and you could see what you were headed into. It didn't deter our bombardier, Lieutenant Hester. He dropped his bombs and the other planes dropped theirs. The bomb bay doors were right in front of me, and I could always watch the bombs. I watched them fall all the way. It seemed like Hester hit the factory itself. The whole target was well plastered and the smoke rose high. Lieutenant Darrow was still clinging on. I knew it wouldn't be long before the fighters returned. The tension was very great.

"Fifteen minutes later, the fighters were sighted coming in from our right. I thought, this is it. I never thought I'd make it back that day. I was really scared, and I prayed to God to get me through this. They circled us once, lined up, and attacked head-on again. Chutes were going down all over the sky, brown ones and white ones: it looked like an airborne invasion. The fighters kept on coming in, passing under and coming around again. The odds were against us. It's not like in the movies, when you hear the fighters zooming and all the sound effects. You just hear your own airplane and its engines. And you hear your own guns.

"At last the fighters left us. We flew on for about fifteen more minutes, then I saw fighters miles to our left and heading our way. We said 'Uh, oh, here we go again,' but they turned out to be our escort. They were angels from heaven. I turned the turret around: there were ten planes left in the group. Lieutenant Darrow was dragging along on two engines, and dropping out to our left. It looked like he would have to ditch in the Channel. The white cliffs of Dover were the most beautiful sight in the world, and ten minutes later, when I got out of the turret, I was the happiest person in all the world. *Big Time Operator* had pulled us through again. We were safe and back in good old England."

The German fighter planes had shot down twenty-one B-17s en route to the target, and destroyed fourteen more on the homeward flight. Although the target defenses were described by seasoned crews as negligible, yet another bomber fell to the Schweinfurt flak. The Eighth had lost more aircraft in a day than in its first six months of operations.

That night Air Chief Marshal Harris sent six hundred heavies to attack the Baltic rocket base at Peenemünde. It was the opening gambit in the Allied air campaign, later code-named Crossbow, which would be waged against the factories and launching sites of the enemy's "V-weapons."

The 4th Bomb Wing, returning from North Africa seven days later and attacking Bordeaux on the way, was grievously depleted. In addition to the aircraft lost attacking Regensburg, another twelve had suffered damage beyond the resources of the African outposts to repair, and three were missing from the shuttle operation over France. For its fight against the odds,

above: A Bristol-powered
Lancaster flying on one
engine; below: A new B-24
Liberator.

below left: Colonel Dale O. Smith, who commanded
the 384th Bomb Group at Grafton Underwood; below:
The nose gear of this B-24 collapsed on landing.

73

The badly wounded Eighth Air Force Bomber Command
was saved in late 1943 by the arrival in England of the
North American P-51 Mustang long-range escort fighters.

The Eighth could no longer sustain the heavy losses in crews and aircraft it was suffering by late 1943. It desperately needed the protection of a fighter escort able to accompany its bombers all the way to the farthest German targets and back to their English bases. That protection came in the form of the Mustang and, to a lesser extent, the Republic P-47 Thunderbolt, far lower left. The P-47 was highly capable and rugged, but the Mustang alone saved the Combined Day/Night Bombing Offensive of the British and American air forces in World War Two.

the whole wing received a Distinguished Unit Citation, and Major Gale Cleven of the 100th Bomb Group, leading the rear formation, which had borne the brunt of the enemy attacks, was awarded the Distinguished Service Cross.

Throughout the dire Regensburg and Schweinfurt operations, the conduct of the crews could not be criticized: they had met the fighter onslaught with enormous courage. The Flying Fortress gunners had hit back with everything they had, and although the early claims were optimistic, as they often could be in the heat of battle (a Messerschmitt came in, many guns were fired at it, and, at the debriefing, several gunners claimed the kill), twenty-five of their attackers had been shot out of the sky. Both the main targets had been accurately bombed, but so efficient were the Germans at rehabilitation that the factories resumed production in a week and were almost back to normal in two months.

Assessed therefore, as bombing operations, the attacks could be looked upon as qualified successes: in terms of economy in men and machinery, they could not be so regarded. Five hundred young Americans were missing in action somewhere over Europe, and many home-coming aircraft had carried dead and wounded. Over thirty-one percent of the bombers had been lost, and others had suffered heavy battle damage. These were savage blows—as savage as any the RAF had taken in the early days—and the Eighth reverted to short-range targets for a while. The next big encounter with the enemy defenses came on September 6, and was as costly as the last. The aiming point in Stuttgart was hidden under cloud, few crews found the primary target, and forty-five aircraft were lost in the attempt. Five more, with battle damage, were forced to land in Switzerland; another twenty-one, short of fuel, ditched or crash-landed in England.

Again, the Eighth stepped back and took a breath. For a few weeks, most of the targets selected for the bombers were in France or on the German North Sea coast. In the next four thousand sorties ninety planes were lost, and a third of these went down on the only long-range mission: an attack on Münster's railways and canals. Eaker then decided that General Anderson's bombers must return to Schweinfurt and its ball-bearing plants. On October 14, the crews were briefed for the follow-up attack. At Great Ashfield, Lieutenant Colonel Vandervanter spoke a few words of encouragement to the 385th Bomb Group. "This is a tough job," he told 'Van's Valiants', "but I know you can do it. Good luck, good bombing, good hunting . . ." From the seated ranks in the briefing room, a lone voice added ". . . and good-bye."

The 1st and 3rd Bomb Divisions dispatched three hundred B-17s to the primary target, while B-24s of the 2nd Bomb Division made a diversionary attack on Emden. Ray Wild was flying his third mission out of Podington with the 92nd Bomb Group. "We were off to an early start. We reached altitude and got over the French coast. Somehow, we failed to pick up the low group of our wing. As we were lead wing, the colonel decided we had better fall in with another group. We did a three-sixty over the Channel and, seeing fifteen planes ahead of us that didn't seem to be attached to anyone, we just tagged along with them. We picked up enemy fighters at just about the time our own escort had to leave. From that moment it was unbelievable.

"For three hours over enemy territory, we had fighters shooting tracer and rockets at us. You could see those rockets coming. They were about eighteen inches long, and when they hit they would explode and set the plane on fire. Some twin-engine jobs at about a thou-

left: The vigil of gathering at the end of a mission to greet the returning airmen; below: The palpable relief at being back on the ground and safe in England after flying another mission to Germany.

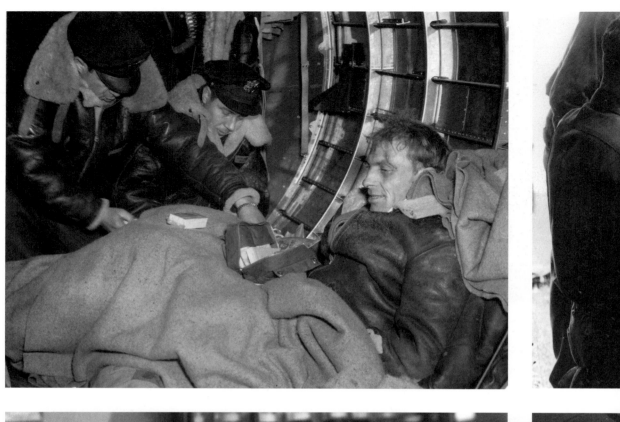

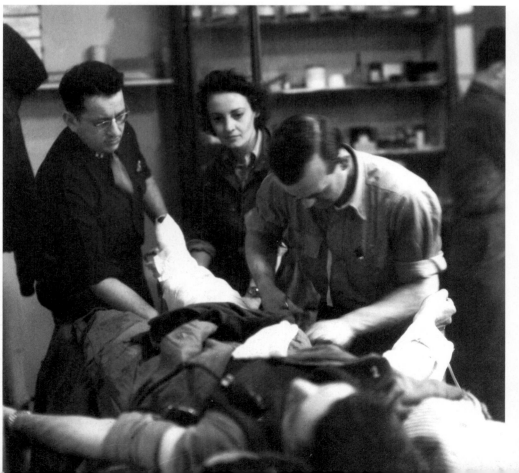

The reality of the air war is literally brought home to the British and American air bases by the B-17s and B-24s carrying their dead and wounded airmen.

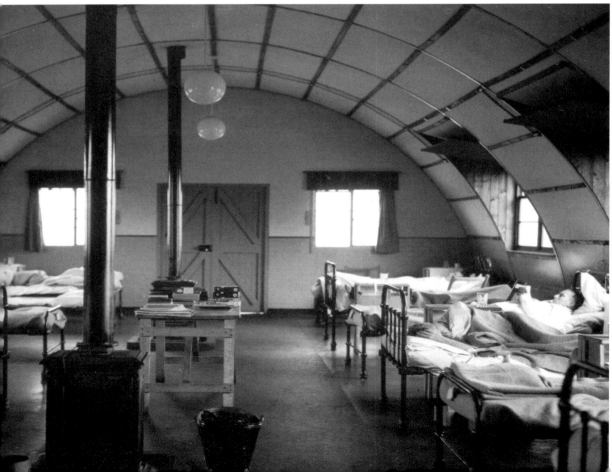

sand feet above us were dropping bombs on the formation. There was no way they could aim at any one bomber—they were just dropping bombs into the group. And they were dropping chains or cables to foul our propellers.

"We were riding Ray Clough's left wing when he got hit. He dropped out and twenty seconds later he burst into flames. Brown got hit and disintegrated: a great sheet of flame and then a hole in the formation. I took over the lead of the second element just prior to going over the target. Major Ott was riding on three engines and had to drop behind. I never saw him again. Even over the target, the fighters came on through the flak. It was one of the few times they did that. They were really first team, those guys. They had guts and they were damned good fliers. They'd come in close, and if you straggled by as much as fifty yards, you'd had it. You'd get hit by three or four guys.

"The main thing was, the lead bombardier did a beautiful job on the target, but about three minutes later we got hit in number three engine. Due to loss of the prop governor control we couldn't feather it, and we began to sweat. We had to use maximum manifold pressure and 2,500 revs to stay in formation. We limped home as far as the Channel and started to let down into the nearest field. We got into Biggin Hill, southeast of London. Seven Forts set down there and they were all shot up. Several had wounded aboard and one had a dead navigator. We had fifteen holes in the ship and only about sixty gallons of gas left. After Schweinfurt, I thought the rest would seem easy."

The return to Schweinfurt had been yet another calamitous event: sixty B-17s had failed to return, more than twice that number had suffered battle damage, and over six hundred officers and men were missing, dead, or wounded.

It could have been a deathblow for precision daylight bombing; indeed, a partial switch to night bombing was considered for a while. At the end of the day, however, the USAAF commanders held fast to their philosophy, while the operations staff at Pinetree undertook a total tactical reappraisal. Stuttgart had indicated the need for pathfinder aircraft, equipped with a version—a better one if possible—of the RAF's H2S radar; all the long-range missions had shown a requirement for more firepower for the bombers and protection for the crews; the combat box formations must be flown tighter for mutual support; above all, the range of the "little friends" had to be extended. Meanwhile, in Germany, the armaments ministry planned a wider dispersal of vital war industries and the urgent construction of underground factories. The Luftwaffe generals had also read the signs: despite their fearful losses, the American formations were still hitting targets and knocking down fighters, and it seemed they intended to go on. There was only one thing for it: Berlin must be told that the production of fighters should immediately be doubled, and that the training hours for pilots had to be reduced.

All these decisions, in England and in Germany, were translated into action in the ensuing months, and those that affected the USAAF fighters' range and the Luftwaffe training were to have a major impact on the outcome of the war. Four months later, in what was to become known as the Eighth Air Force's "Big Week," Schweinfurt was to discover what bombing round the clock meant. On February 24, 1944, the 1st Air Division, heavily escorted by P-47s and the new Merlin-engined P-51 Mustangs, all with long-range fuel tanks, struck the ball-bearing plants. That same night, Air Chief Marshal Harris, pausing briefly in the Battle of Berlin, dispatched his Lancasters and Halifaxes in two separate attacks with two thousand tons of bombs. The whirlwind had come, and the dead had been avenged.

The enormity of the experience they have just had over Germany is evident in the faces of this Fortress crew, and those airmen gathered at the Red Cross mobile canteen for coffee and doughnuts.

WESTERN UNION

1281

This is a full-rate Telegram or Cablegram unless its deferred character is indicated by a suitable symbol above or preceding the address.

A. N. WILLIAMS
PRESIDENT

NEWCOMB CARLTON
CHAIRMAN OF THE BOARD

J. C. WILLEVER
FIRST VICE-PRESIDENT

(58)==

DL=Day Letter
NT=Overnight Telegram
LC=Deferred Cable
NLT=Cable Night Letter
Ship Radiogram

The filing time shown in the date line on telegrams and day letters is STANDARD TIME at point of origin. Time of receipt is STANDARD TIME at point of destination

LB305W (TWO) 46 GOVT=PXXWMUB WASHINGTON DC 30 551P=
DEC 30 PM 6 17

MRS CECELIA MCCARREN=
10 PARROTT ST (LYNN MASS)=

THE SECRETARY OF WAR DESIRES ME TO EXPRESS HIS DEEP REGRET
THAT YOUR SON STAFF SERGEANT WILLIAM R MCCARREN HAS BEEN
REPORTED MISSING IN ACTION SINCE TWENTY DECEMBER IN EUROPEAN
AREA PERIOD IF FURTHER DETAILS OR OTHER INFORMATION ARE
RECEIVED YOU WILL BE PROMPTLY NOTIFIED PERIOD=
ULIO THE ADJUTANT GENERAL.

left: Staff Sergeant William McCarren was the radio-gunner of a B-17 of the 379th Bomb Group based at Kimbolton, England. His plane was hit by German flak and he baled out, was captured and became a prisoner of war, along with many thousands of American and British airmen of WW2. He survived the experience and ultimately wrote an amazing account of it; right: A still from the 1963 film *The Great Escape* with Steve McQueen (pictured), Richard Attenborough, and James Garner. Stalag Luft III, the site of the real 'Great Escape,' was located near Sagan, Silesia, and was home to more than 10,000 British and American airmen who had become prisoners of the Germans in the war years. It was probably the largest and best known of the many German military prison camps in the Second World War.

An unfortunate aspect of the air war was that many of the participating aircraft were so badly damaged by flak or fighters that, if they made it back to an airfield in England, they had to execute and, hopefully, survive a belly-landing. Here are some examples of such incidents, this particular one happened to the B-17G, *Little Miss Mischief*, of the 91st Bomb Group stationed at Bassingbourn.

This is the result of a horrendous ground accident rather than a belly-landing.

above: A meeting at the combat mess hall after a mission; left: The chow line queue at Deenethorpe, wartime home to the 401st Bomb Group.

Prewar RAF stations were compact, brick-built settlements set close by the airfields, with neat, paved roads, squash courts and tennis courts, playing fields and cinemas, workshops and barber shops, canteens and libraries, churches and sick bays; the great "C" type hangars, standing in a phalanx, held not only aircraft but centrally-heated offices and comfortable crew rooms. You approached these bases along a tree-lined avenue, through guarded, wrought-iron gates, to arrive at the proud, grey edifice of Station Headquarters, with an RAF ensign fluttering above. The three-storey messes, with ivy-covered walls, fronted by flower beds, offered spacious dining rooms, ante-rooms, billiard rooms, ladies' rooms, and quiet rooms. You would not have been terribly surprised to find a butler's pantry. A few British, Canadian, and Australian squadrons lived on bases of this sort, and American fighter groups occupied a handful, but the only USAAF bomb groups so comfortably ensconced were the 91st at Bassingbourn near Cambridge and, at a later time, the 458th at Horsham St Faith near Norwich.

Other bases were thrown up in a hurry to accommodate the majority of Eighth Air Force bomb groups, and to meet the expansion of both the Allied bomber commands in 1943. They were technically functional, but their facilities were primitive and their aspect was austere. They were grafted onto fields where, only week before, farmers had grazed cattle or raised potatoes, wheat, and barley. Their narrow roads were muddy, and the only structures over ten feet high were the control tower, the water tower, the A.M. Bombing Teacher, the parachute store, and the far-flung "T-2" hangars (no crew rooms or heating) on the fringes of the field. All the other buildings were prefabricated huts and shanty-type structures dispersed around the area as though they had been taken up and dropped as an example of saturation bombing at its worst. Strangely, many airmen preferred this type of base: perhaps it just seemed better suited to the waging of a war.

Sam Burchell's base at Seething was of the wartime sort. "Our building was a Nissen hut—just one big room for about forty of us, with one stove in the middle for which we were always trying to steal coal. It was extremely cold in the winter in that part of England, and damp. There were no separate quarters for sergeants or anything like that. Actually, everybody in the Air Force was a sergeant except me."

Of his quarters at Lissett, RAF rear gunner Fred Allen said: "We lived in a wooden hut beside a hedge two miles from the camp. There were four crews to a hut—twenty-eight people—and you got to know them pretty well. You didn't get to know many others. You slept, you flew, and the only time you weren't with your crew was when you went on leave."

When the B-24 crews of the 467th Bomb Group arrived at Rackheath in early March of 1944, the airfield contractors were still working on the base. The group was destined to fly over five thousand sorties, and to achieve the highest overall rating for accurate bombing in the Eighth; initially, however, it took a little while to get things organized. "Our squadron is running this postal deal like an Easter egg hunt," Keith Newhouse noted in his diary. "One day we get the mail at the officers' club, one time at the intelligence officer's room, then the medics have it, and today we pick it up at the MP gate. I hope someone can fall on the solution of one man taking care of it at one place and each man calling for his own. But that's so simple the powers that be will never think of it."

Sergeant Ira Eakin's first assignment, in July 1942, was to a fighter training field at Atcham, recently vacated by the RAF; Eakin next moved to Abbotts Ripton, repairing damaged

far left: Herding turkeys for Thanksgiving Day dinner at an air base of the Eighth Air Force; left: A 'rest home' for flak-happy airmen lucky enough to be sent there for a week of respite from the war; bottom left: Thanksgiving dinner served at Great Ashfield in November 1943; bottom right: Audley End Station, where thousands of American airmen caught trains on their forty-eight-hour leaves to London.

There were occasional visits by celebrities to the airfields of the Eighth, this one by film star Leslie Howard, who played Spitfire designer R.J. Mitchell in *The First of The Few.*

Fortresses and Liberators, and then as a ground crew chief with the 91st Bomb Group at Bassingbourn, where he compared the amenities unfavorably with those he had earlier enjoyed. "On the main part of the base they had brick barrack blocks, but we were over the road in little Quonset huts with coke burners and double-deck bunks. I never did know this for a fact, but it was rumored that they gave the mess officer a medal for feeding more troops on less chow than anybody in Europe. We got two meals a day. Breakfast was about ten o'clock and consisted usually of marmalade and that sawdust bread and powdered eggs and a cup of hot tea; then about three o'clock we had lamb—well, it started off as lamb chops and two or three days later it would come back as a stew. By the time the stew came around you could smell it a quarter of a mile from the mess hall. I never did care for lamb to begin with. Man, that was the lousiest chow."

Initially, Keith Newhouse was equally unhappy with the food at Rackheath. "It has gradually improved, but it surely isn't interesting. We get some whole eggs, and steak once in ten days. The Eighth must have bought the entire U.S. output of orange marmalade, and we get our quota of Spam and powdered eggs. No fresh milk. Coffee has a peculiar green coloring. One new experience is mustard: it is a bland yellow in color, doesn't smell strong, so a liberal first helping is taken. After the flame has cleared away and the smoke stops coming up the windpipe, the victim learns a healthy respect for it. It has no taste, just heat."

Although Spam—the ubiquitous spiced ham—was pallid fare, with little taste of ham and none of spice, most mess hall menus, British and American, tended to include it. Spam frit-

Pin-ups adorn this 8AF Nissen hut.

ters were not at all unpleasant, and the cooks at Kimbolton even held a competition in preparing Spam dishes gourmet style.

Either Ken Stone was less critical than his fellow airmen or, as one who was so skinny on enlistment that he had to eat three bananas and drink four pints of water to meet the weight requirement, he needed more sustenance. In general, he approved of the meals at Ridgewell. "The food was good—regular meat and potatoes. The only thing I wouldn't eat was liver. I hated that. But you could go to the Red Cross Aero Club and get a snack and a Coke anytime. Some of the crew drank beer, but I was too young for that. I didn't care about liquor. I got drunk once, on our first leave, but that was the only time I did. We had movies on the base or in town, and dances. I was shy with girls, and I didn't dance. I was a drummer, so I just stood and watched the drummers all the time. I bought a bike and painted it white, and got around on that. We'd bicycle to Halstead and back, and that was good exercise."

Lawrence Drew recalled a minor fracas in his Nissen hut at Grafton Underwood: "The people playing poker had the lights on and they would play all night. An officer said, 'Come on fellas, have a heart—some guys have got to fly tomorrow.' They just said something back to him and went right on playing, so he took a forty-five from the head of his bed, and walked down the line and shot all those lights out. We had it dark in there after that—for the rest of the night anyway."

Colonel Dale O. Smith found the food at Grafton Underwood less than exciting when he arrived to take command. Seeking an improvement, he sent three mess cooks to study the techniques of hotel chefs in London; next he used an aircraft starter motor to power a liquidizer for converting powdered eggs and milk into a palatable mixture; finally, he obtained an ice cream factory, that was locally abandoned, and set it up on base. Free ice cream for every patron doubled the movie attendance overnight.

It was natural that British airmen, inured to years of rationing, should find little to complain of in the service diet. The quality might leave something to be desired—no mess cook could prepare a meal the way that mother did—but quantities were adequate and more. "I thought it was good," said Tony Partridge of the food at Snaith. "I can't remember having a poor meal. We always had eggs, bacon, and sausage before we went on an op—perhaps that was why we never felt hungry, even on a ten-hour trip."

There were few formal party nights for round-the-clock bomber men, either in RAF messes or Eighth Air Force clubs. Most of the parties occurred spontaneously—somebody's birthday, a promotion, a crew's end of tour, or just because it seemed like a good idea at the time. There would be singing, possibly dancing, probably some beer-drinking races and games—which were quite likely to become increasingly boisterous as the night went on. RAF men traditionally indulged in "High Cockalorum," "Are You There, Moriarty," "Do You Know The Muffin Man," and building human pyramids. American fliers had their own ideas of fun, and since they were far from the comforts of home, these tended to include a feminine element. "English women," said Sidney Rapoport, "were brought in by the truckload. It was a huge novelty to them, because of the great expanse of food, the beverages—and, of.

VE Day is celebrated at the Glatton control tower, 8 May 1945; right: Touch football at Kimbolton.

course, the gaiety." It was a time for relaxing, for putting footprints on the ceiling, for calling colonels by their first names and maybe for getting just a little drunk. When a USAAF bomb group flew its hundredth mission, the base might celebrate with a three-day stand-down. "I wormed my way into the 'hundred party' of the 91st," said Rapoport. "Everybody let their hair down. I saw Doolittle and Eaker in a race, trying to push pennies across the floor with their noses. It sure was wild."

Like many young Americans, Calvin A. Swaffer had seen the writing on the wall some months before the Japanese attacked Pearl Harbor. He had enlisted in the Royal Canadian Air Force. He learned to fly, and transferred to the USAAF in 1942. Between October of that year and the following August he flew twenty-five missions as pilot of The *Memphis Blues*, a B-17 of the 303rd Bomb Group at Molesworth in Huntingdonshire. "The four officers on our crew slept in one room," he remembered, and we had no heat in it at all. I slept under seven blankets."

A normal breakfast, in Swaffer's experience, would be of powdered eggs (the fliers called them "square eggs"), and the occasional pancake, but on mission mornings there would be the fresh egg for each man. Other meals consisted principally of Spam, mutton, and Brussels sprouts. "I spent days on end with nothing to do but get up, go to mess, and play games at the officers' club such as Ping-Pong, blackjack, hearts, and checkers, with now and then being called out to fly a combat mission. The club was used by two squadrons. It had a huge fireplace, a games room, and a bar. A whole lot of beer and booze was consumed, especially

With their lives on hold for
the duration of the war, the
350,000 Americans of the
Eighth Air Force shared some
of their infrequent spare time
with their British friends.

Entertaining local children was a part of life on the airfields of the Eighth.

after a raid."

The officers' club was not a venue highly favored by John B. Thomas, Jr., who flew thirty-five missions as copilot of a B-24 with the 446th at Flixton. "It was usually full of base types and we had to fly too much to hang around a lot of permanent poker games and barflies. On a three-day pass, we would take off for Norwich or London."

Calvin Swaffer was another who did not confine his leisure moments to the base. "We got to visit Thrapston, Kettering, and Northampton, and the pubs were great. I learned to drink the warm, dark beer called Bitter, and play darts. I also got to visit London several times. The most impressive thing was the blackout—the torches people carried around with them, and the 'Underground' they slept in when the German bombers came over. Of course, the British Museum was also impressive, what with the Rosetta stone and the Magna Carta and a lot of other real good stuff. There were tea dances at the Piccadilly Hotel every afternoon, where you would meet officers from all the free countries of western Europe. It was great to meet all those nice people, and, above all, the young ladies." Among all his experiences, however, Swaffer maintained that his biggest thrill was having tea at Buckingham Palace with his commanding general as guests of their Majesties the King and Queen of England. When the war was over, Swaffer flew on as an airline pilot until he reached the age of sixty. He completed 28,500 flying hours, and never had an accident.

Depending on the operational requirements, most RAF crews could expect a fair amount of leave: one week in six was the normal allocation, with the prospect of at least another week at the end of tour. Free rail passes were provided for six journeys a year, and Lord Nuffield, the Morris automobile magnate, made funds available for every man to spend a week at a hotel of his choice. For the Eighth Air Force crews, furloughs were usually of shorter duration, with a longer mid-tour break at a rest and recuperation center—a "flak farm"—located in one of the quieter and less war-torn regions of the English countryside.

Of his stretch at Horsham St Faith, Charles Bosshardt remembered that he never seemed to get enough sleep. "They would get us up anywhere from one to five a.m. and a high percentage of our missions were scrubbed for weather, and then we flew practice missions or were test-hopping or going to ground classes. Any free time we did have, we slept as late as we could." Of that winter's weather, he particularly recalled "the worst fog I ever encountered. It froze on the branches and made them look like Christmas trees, sprayed. You could only see about fifty feet in front of you and, being strange to the base, we had to have help from other guys to find the mess hall."

An American Raid

As recalled by Sergeant Roger Armstrong, radio/gunner, 91st Bomb Group, Bassingbourn; I felt a tug on my shoulder and before I could open my eyes and come out of the wonderful dream I was having, someone tugged again. He put his mouth close to my ear and shone a flashlight in my face. I realized I was not in Sioux Falls, necking with a beautiful brunette in Sherman Park. I was in the 401st Squadron barracks at Bassingbourn, looking at the duty corporal. "Breakfast at 0300" he said, "briefing at 0400, stations at 0515." And he was gone.

I shouldn't have been surprised. The day before, on October 14, 1944, we had dropped "nickels" on Cologne; among them were copies of *The Stars and Stripes* printed in German, with a message to the Luftwaffe from General Doolittle, calling them a bunch of cowards and challenging them to a battle over Cologne the next day. Hilmer Beicker, our flight engineer, was born of German parents in Houston, Texas, and he had read the whole thing out to us over the intercom. We had all pitied the crews who would be going on the next day's

Sergeant Roger Armstrong, radio-gunner, 91st Bomb Group, Bassingbourn.

Contact with a friendly American female in the person of a Red Cross mobile canteen worker.

mission after an insult like that.

While brushing my teeth, I admired the clean, yellow tiling in our latrine, and I thought how lucky we were to be stationed at a permanent base built by the Royal Air Force in 1938. The latrines were never crowded and we had central heating, so no battles with pot-bellied stoves like we had in basic training.

As I dressed quickly in a suntan shirt and old OD pants, I couldn't help feeling fear, deep inside. I was ashamed to admit that I was afraid, but I found in later years that you weren't normal unless you had that feeling. It was really dark when I went outside. I tested the temperature and put on my fur-collared B10 jacket. My bike was in a rack outside the door, but the light batteries were dead so I had to steer with one hand, with a flashlight in the other, as I rode to the combat mess hall. All the combat crews ate at the combat mess so the Air Force could control the types of food we ate. Nothing was fed to us on mission days that would cause gas in the stomach or the intestinal tract, because the gas would expand as your plane climbed to altitude. No one liked the powdered eggs, especially when there were green spots on them. There was a large grill outside the serving line where we could fry eggs to our taste. We purchased our own eggs from the farmer whose backyard was right behind the hardstand of our B-17. When the pilot or the crew chief ran the engines up, the prop wash struck the chicken coops and the feathers really flew. We could never figure out how those hens could lay with all that going on. When the farmer was out of hen eggs, we would buy his duck eggs out of desperation, to avoid those horrible green and yellow powdered eggs.

After breakfast, we drifted over to the briefing building, the only Quonset hut on the base. It was a king-size hut because it had to seat thirty-six or thirty-seven crews. There was a mission map of the British Isles and the Continent on a large board set on the stage, with a curtain hung over it. I sat down with Hilmer and the rest of my crew: the pilot, John Askins, came from Oakland, California; the copilot, Randall Archer, from Chester, West Virginia; the navigator, Anthony Delaporta, from Philadelphia, Pennsylvania; the bombardier, Paul Collier, from Hamilton, Texas; the waist gunner/armorer, Ralph Azevedo, from Mill Valley, California; the ball turret gunner, Robert Webb, from Dyer, Tennessee; and the tail gunner, Roy Loyless, from Houston, Texas.

I noted that the time was just 0400. Right on cue, one of the Headquarters officers barked, "Tenshut." Colonel Terry walked in at a brisk pace, stepped onto the stage and said, "At ease, gentlemen." He gave us a pep talk and turned the briefing over to the S-2 intelligence officer.

The S-2 walked over to the map, carrying his pool stick, and pulled the curtain up ever so slowly, as if he savored every moment of the anxiety he was causing in his audience. The red yarn indicated we were going to Cologne, and the reaction was a moan, which gradually crescendoed. The target was the marshaling yards, and we were to disrupt the supplies of armor, artillery, and troops to Aachen, where our soldiers were fighting. There were pieces of red plastic on the map which represented the areas of heavy flak. It bothered us that the S-2 officer would sometimes shift those pieces around, as though he wasn't sure of where those concentrations were. We all knew they were around the large cities; the problem was that no one knew how much mobile flak had been moved into the target area on flatbed train cars.

The weather officer said that the cloud over England was about 19,000 feet thick, but not too bad over the Continent. The operations officer gave a time hack so we could set our watches to Greenwich Mean Time, and then we were dismissed. On the way out, we had to pass the three chaplains. Now, I didn't particularly want to be reminded that I might soon meet my Maker, so as we passed I looked the other way. When we got into the fresh air I realized how warm a room could get when the men in there all became concerned about what fate might hold for them that day.

There were other briefings for the pilot, copilot, navigator, bombardier, and me. I reported to the communications building to pick up the codes of the day, the verification codes that were sent when messages were transmitted or received. The communications officer gave me an aluminum briefcase containing the codes, along with log sheets and pencils for recording my messages while on the mission. The codes were printed on rice paper so you could eat them if you were shot down. The officer mentioned that the Germans broke most of our codes within twelve hours. I was given the colors of the day for the Very lights (flares), which we fired when passing over a convoy or a naval vessel so they wouldn't mistake us for a German plane.

In the equipment room, we collected our Mae Wests, parachutes and harness, oxygen masks, headsets and throat mikes, goggles, gabardine coveralls, heated suits, leather helmets and steel helmets with earflaps that covered your headset. There were heated felt inserts to go inside the sheepskin and leather flying boots, and silk gloves to wear inside the heated leather gloves. We stowed the gear in our equipment bags, and then we picked up the escape kits, which contained a silk map, a razor, high-energy candy, a plastic bottle, water purification tablets, and translation sheets in Flemish, Dutch, French, and German.

They had taken photos of us when we arrived at the base, which you were to give to the Resistance if you got shot down, so they could make you an identity document. I never took my photos along (a chief German interrogator told me recently that they could tell your bomb group by the civilian coat you were wearing the day they took your photo). We didn't take the .45-caliber Colt automatics along, either, because the S-2 had found the possession of a gun had given the Germans an excuse to shoot you.

It was a five-minute ride in a six-by-six truck from the hangar to the dispersal area where our B-17, *The Qualified Quail*, was parked. We all had our own thoughts and everyone was quiet on the way. It was a gray, depressing morning, and the overcast was down to 100 or

New Boeing B-17Gs at an air depot in England.

150 feet. The driver stopped in front of our plane. It carried the markings of the triangle "A" on the tail and our squadron letter "K." The wingtips, tail plane, and stabilizer were painted red, which indicated we were in the 1st Combat Wing. The markings helped the group to assemble and then to find our wing. We all looked in the bomb bay to see what kind of bombs we were carrying: if you carried delayed-action bombs, you had to take off anyway, even if the weather changed, and drop them in the North Sea. We had a full load of 250-pound bombs and two clusters of M-17 incendiaries on the top shackles.

I put my heated suit on over my coveralls, and this was a mistake, because as soon as I climbed into the plane to check out the radio room, I always got the call of nature. As usual, I found a semi-secluded spot to take care of that. At the same time, I could hear Beicker throwing up. He said, "I don't know why, but once I enter the waist door and smell the interior of the plane, I get sick at my stomach." I told him not to worry about it. It was that smell—of oil, gas, canvas flak suits, and ammunition boxes.

In the radio room, I checked the spare chest-type chute pack, the walk-around oxygen bottle, and the four-by-four piece of armor plating the crew chief had found for me. My radios and rack of frequency ranges were all in place, and so was the frequency meter, in case I needed to check the accuracy of what a dial on the receiver read.

John and Randy, with Beicker and the crew chief, checked the exterior and interior of the plane, while the gunners checked their guns and ammunition. When the engines were started, I heard them cough and splutter before they started to run. We put on our headsets and checked the intercom, and then John ran the engines up while the ground crew stood by with fire extinguishers. The plane vibrated and became very noisy. I heard the sound of the brakes being released as John moved onto the taxiway and fell in behind the ship we were to follow in the line for takeoff. I turned on my radios and the IFF. I would monitor the Division frequency during the mission: the IFF would send a continuous code while we were over friendly territory so the coastal defenses wouldn't shoot at us.

The lead squadron took off at 0600, and by 0622 all twelve were airborne. John turned onto the runway and ran the engines while he held the brakes on. The plane kind of jerked into a rolling start as he released them. Runway 25 was 6,000 feet long, but it seemed he was never going to lift that heavy load off as we gathered speed. Then the plane broke loose from the pull of gravity and we were airborne. I noticed I had held myself stiff while we were moving down that runway, but now I relaxed. Watching out of the radio room window by my desk, I saw we were higher than the village church steeple, then suddenly we were in the overcast and flying blind.

John had to fly at a given speed and rate of climb for so many minutes, then turn right, still climbing, and turn again so we were making one big square around the Bassinbourn Buncher beacon. It was quite nerve-racking in the overcast. It was so thick, I could barely see the left wingtip. A voice on the intercom said, "Submarine at nine o'clock level." No one answered. The plane bounced around and we knew it was from the prop wash of another B-17 out there somewhere.

Randy's voice came over the intercom: "Copilot to crew, we are passing through 10,000 feet, so oxygen masks on, please." A few minutes later he said, "Oxygen check," and we answered to our names from tail to nose: "Loyless okay," "Azevedo okay," "Webb okay," and finally "Collier okay."

Developed by Boeing in the 1930s, the B-17 four-engined heavy bomber resulted from a competition with Douglas and Martin to build 200 new bombers for the US Army Air Corps. Boeing lost the competition when its prototype crashed on a test flight, but the Air Corps was so impressed with the plane that it ordered additional examples and the B-17 went into full production to become the principal U.S. strategic bomber for much of the war, until it was superceded by the Boeing B-29, the aircraft that dropped the atomic bombs on Japan.

We broke out of the overcast for a few minutes, and saw twenty or thirty B-17s around us. The third squadron from the 91st was just below us. Then, we were climbing back into the cloud, still making squares over the base Buncher. Finally it began to look a little lighter and we popped out of the mess. We were to fly high squadron of the group, and the group was to lead the 1st Combat Wing, with one wing ahead of us. Collier saw the lead squadron forming up and we located our element leader of the high squadron. It was still hazy, but with just sufficient visibility to get the group formed, and we set course for Clacton at 20,000 feet. The 381st and 398th Bomb Groups had taken off after us, and our group leader did a series of "S" turns to let them catch up and form the combat wing.

We left Clacton two minutes early at an altitude of 21,000 feet. The winds over the Channel were greater than briefed, and John told Tony, the navigator, that the whole wing was doing another S turn because we were catching up on the wing ahead of us. We were at 27,000 feet when we arrived at point two on the route to Cologne, still two minutes early but with everyone spaced at normal intervals. Over the bomber channel I heard the weather ship, *Buckeye Blue*, report that the route weather was good but that contrails were forming at the bombers' altitude. Then *Buckeye Red* said that Cologne was overcast and that the PFF ships would be needed to locate and zero in on the target with radar.

Out over the Channel, just before we reached the Continent, the gunners had test-fired their guns. They had charged their guns before we reached high altitude, because the barrel shrank at low temperature, and if you didn't have a shell in it, the gun probably wouldn't fire.

As we flew toward Cologne, Tony called John and said: "We're running parallel to the front lines; that's why we can see flak up ahead." I thought, why aren't we flying on the Allied side, instead of over the German lines? Meantime, I was copying a message for the wing commander in the lead ship, from the 1st Air Division. There were about a dozen German ground operators jamming the frequency, but Division was sending the Morse on a modulated tone that sounded like a big truck horn honking. You soon got used to that tone, and the jamming

didn't really bother you.

We had put our flak suits on as we entered German territory, and I snapped the chest pack on the right ring of my harness. It left an area vulnerable, but I felt the chute would absorb low-velocity flak or even a bullet fired at long range. Suddenly the plane rose and fell four or five times. There was flak below us, not doing any damage but it was worrying me. I concentrated on copying some of the German code, because the busier you were the less you thought about getting hit, but they were just holding their keys down or tapping out a series of V's. I lost interest and got back to trying to get rid of the ache in my chest, thinking about the curtains of flak we would be going through at Cologne.

The wing commander started a series of S turns to throw the German gunners off, and John told us what was happening. We all felt John was the best pilot in the group, and he was also a good communicator. He always advised what was going on. We in turn watched out from our positions and told him if we noticed a mechanical or structural problem with the airplane.

I listened in on the group voice channel and heard the pilot of the lead PFF ship in the low squadron say, "We have lost our bombing radar." The lead command ship said, "Drop on our smoke bombs at the target."

We were getting both tracking flak and box barrage flak as we flew past Cologne to the

To succeed in the daylight bombing campaign against Germany, Eighth Bomber Command needed the help of "the Little Friends", the pilots of the new P-51 Mustangs arriving in Britain in large quantities by early 1944.

south and picked up our IP, where we started our run in to the target. The plane was really bouncing up and down, and I moved my piece of armor plating across the radio room to the chaff chute. We were carrying seven cartons of chaff bundles, which were held together by paper strips until they were pushed through the chute and hit the slipstream. Our group would create thousands of false blips on the enemy's radar screens to help the groups behind us, the way the group ahead was helping us. On the right side of the ship, I built up a flak shack of chaff cartons on my armor plating. Webb was too large to wear his flak helmet in the ball turret so he loaned it to me. I pulled my own helmet down over my eyes, placed Webb's over my reproductive organs, and started throwing chaff.

Suddenly the radio room lit up bright red, and the plexiglass roof window blew inward in a thousand pieces with a number of shell fragments. Then another shell exploded just above the nose. We went into a dive, leveled out, and eased back into the formation. What had happened was that a piece of flak had come through the windshield and struck John on the right shoulder of his flak suit, turning him in a clockwise direction and making him chop all four engines with his right hand, which was holding the throttles. Randy had pushed the throttles forward and flown us back into position.

Hilmer Beicker came out of the top turret and saw John struggling to turn himself forward. His seat belt was so tight he was having a tough time, so Beicker went to help him. At that moment Randy reached for his flak helmet and was just putting it on when another piece of flak came through the window and struck him on the head. Beicker stopped him from falling on the yoke, and grabbed the first aid kit. Randy came to, and shook his head as Beicker was wiping the blood out of his eyes. It turned out that the flak had only grazed his forehead.

Beicker took a look at the instruments, looked around the flight deck, and went back to the top turret. There was a hole in the plexiglass and a chunk out of the housing; otherwise the turret was in good shape.

I was just throwing a bundle of chaff out when another close burst, which I heard, sent three pieces through the skin of the plane four or five inches from my head. If I had been reaching for another bundle, my head would have taken all three fragments. The holes peeled outward, so the fragments had come right through the ship. I looked around: the right side of my liaison set had a hole the size of your fist in it.

Another burst hit us, and a piece of flak struck my left glove, ripping the leather open from my wrist to the end of my thumb. I felt the blood get warm on my hand, and visualized the thumb—shot off inside the glove. I didn't want to take the glove off, but I knew I had to because of the bleeding. I was relieved when I saw that the thumb was still attached to my hand. I dumped some sulfa out of the first aid kit on two cuts and put a bandage on. This had kind of held my attention, and I realized that John had been calling on the intercom" "Pilot to Radio, Pilot to Radio." I answered, "Radio to Pilot." "Pilot to Radio—Azevedo is down in the waist. See what's wrong." I grabbed my walk-around oxygen bottle and took off for the waist. Azevedo was lying on his back. I saw him blink, so I knew he was alive. When I squatted down beside him, it was obvious he had been hit in the right thigh. Having checked that his mask was securely connected to the right waist oxygen supply, I disconnected my walk-around bottle and plugged into the left waist hose. I took my Boy Scout knife and cut the leg of his pants open. The hole was the size of a silver dollar. It was bleeding but not pumping blood, so I assumed the fragment had missed the femoral artery.

When I took my gloves off, my fingers stiffened up so they wouldn't function properly. I had to keep putting the gloves on to warm up. It got so bad I called the pilot and told him I needed help. By this time I was feeling a little drunk and I kind of plopped down beside Azevedo on my behind. He kept pointing at the ceiling and I saw that the oxygen line I was plugged into had been sliced in two. I thought, although the flak had eased off, they were still trying to get me, one way or another. I plugged back into the walk-around bottle and after a few deep breaths of pure oxygen I felt normal. It wasn't as good as feeling half-drunk.

Beicker arrived to help, and between the two of us we got a pressure bandage on Azevedo's wound, but the temperature at our altitude did more to stop the bleeding. The copilot called for an oxygen check, and the first on his list didn't answer, so I crawled on back to the tail, lugging the walk-around bottle. I got to Loyless on my hands and knees. His eyes were as big as saucers and he was holding the cord to his mike, which a piece of flak had cut in two, three or four inches from his throat. I plugged into his jack box and told Randy what had happened.

Back at the waist, Beicker had found that the piece of flak had come out at the back of

Most airmen of the daylight bombing campaign feared the deadly, unpredictable, radar-controlled anti-aircraft fire they called flak, especially during their bomb run, when they had to maintain a straight, steady course with no evasive manoeuvres. One recalled: "It came up and exploded looking like a little armless dwarf. A near miss sounded like someone was throwing pebbles at the plane."

Azevedo's thigh. We started all over stopping the blood at that point and putting sulfa on the wound. Then we bandaged him up and put a couple of blankets around his legs. To talk to Beicker I had to take my mask off, yell in his ear, and put the mask back on quick. I yelled, "Maybe we should give him a shot of morphine—he could be going into shock."

Beicker held his cupped hand behind my ear: "I think we should. You give it to him." My medical knowledge was confined to what I had picked up in the Boy Scouts, *Reader's Digest*, and a Red Cross class at Creighton University in the Aviation Cadet program. I yelled back, "I've never given a shot before. Maybe you should do it: you know all about engines and stuff like that."

Beicker's eyes looked kind of funny. "So what? You know all about radios. And you showed me a Red Cross card one time where it said you had qualified for first aid."

Azevedo was lying there and he could hear my side of the conversation in his headset. He kept trying to get our attention, and finally he said, "You guys aren't giving me any dope." I said, "Look Azzie, you haven't got much say in this matter." He said, "Neither one of you guys knows anything about medicine. And when we got our shots at Sioux City, Beicker fainted when the first needle went into his arm."

That was true; they gave him three more shots while he was on the floor. Anyway, I was about to lose my voice from yelling. I took the morphine out of the first aid kit. It looked like a small tube of toothpaste with a needle in the end. I warmed it under my heated suit and aimed the needle at the muscle a few inches from the front hole in his thigh. At first I pushed real easy and it didn't go in. I looked up at Beicker. He looked away. I shoved hard and it slid into the thigh. I squeezed the tube and in a few minutes Azevedo had drifted off to sleep.

I looked out of the window and saw we were still in flak. The plane shook and a burst over the nose knocked the bombardier off his seat. Later, I saw the dent in his helmet, and a lump on his head to match. He crawled back to the bombsight and I heard him say, "Bomb bay doors are opening, follow the PDI." That was the pilot direction indicator on the instrument panel.

The group's bombs were dropped from 27,000 feet at 0928. The clouds had cleared and we were able to see our bombs striking the marshaling yards. John had feathered the numbers one and three engines while we were working on Azevedo. Other planes near us also had engines feathered. John got number one engine started again and we were able to stay with the formation. Several bombers from the lead and low squadrons were straggling behind. On the fighter channel, I heard the lead ship ask for "little friends" to assist the damaged planes.

There was cloud at our altitude when we reached the Channel, and the group let down to get under it. This helped the stragglers to keep up with the formation. The fighter protection was excellent. At 1143 we crossed the English coast at Clacton, and the wing broke up, with each group heading back to its own base, pretty well strung out and flying loose.

I went back every ten minutes to see if Azevedo was okay. I took his pulse to see if maybe he had died, but his heart was beating and his skin was warm. I took his mask off when we were at low altitude. John called me to the flight deck as we approached Bassingbourn, and asked me to load the Very pistol with red/red flares to show he had injuries aboard. Looking out through the broken window I saw a number of planes also firing flares. On the final approach, the tail and ball gunners took their positions in the radio room, and the navigator and bombardier came out of the nose.

The ambulances were lined up on the left of runway 25. As we touched down, one raced along the grass beside the runway, and when we turned off and stopped near the tower, the medics were ready to come aboard and remove Azevedo. Instead of taking him to the base hospital they took him to Wimpole Hall, which was set up to treat the more serious injuries. I was kind of glad they took him there. It had been the home of Rudyard Kipling, who was a favorite in my family. My father used to quote Kipling's poems in his sermons at Sioux Falls.

We left *The Qualified Quail* by the tower with a number of other badly damaged B-17s,

Cologne was the primary target of the Eighth Air Force in the raid that Armstrong has described. They managed to avoid damaging the great Cologne cathedral for the most part; right: The home base of Roger Armstrong's 91st Bomb Group at Bassingbourn, England.

and a truck took us to the interrogation building. We were escorted to a table where the S-2 officer poured double shots of scotch into coffee cups. He wanted to know what we all saw on the mission and asked about our injuries.

Randy was sitting next to me; he had pulled up his jacket sleeve and was pushing at something just under the skin of his arm. It was a metal splinter, about four inches long. He had worked it almost out when the S-2 asked what he was doing. Randy said, "I felt my arm itch. I just found piece of flak in it." He pulled it out all the way and put it in his pocket. The S-2 saw the nicks on his forehead and asked if he wanted to see the flight surgeon. Randy said no, he had a date. I did too. I said I had treated my cut hand in the plane. John didn't mention the bruise on his shoulder; he told me later it was sore for three weeks.

After interrogation we took a look at *The Qualified Quail*. After finding two hundred holes we got tired of counting. John, Beicker and the crew chief were looking at something under the right wing. As I walked up, John said, "Our main spar was almost shot in two. If I had known about it, I wouldn't have banked so steep, and I would have taken it easier coming in for landing." It turned out that of thirty-six B-17s of the 91st Bomb Group, sixteen sustained minor damage and twenty had major damage. We had an excellent lunch of steak and potatoes, with ice cream for dessert. I took a shower and went into Royston where I met my date. We did some pub-crawling, and the next morning I slept in as we didn't fly a mission. Two days later, they sent us back to Cologne.

The most famous aircraft associ-
ated with the Bassingbourn-based
91st Bomb Group was the
Memphis Belle, one of the first
B-17s to complete its twenty-five
combat mission-tour of duty in
the Second World War. The *Belle*
is restored and displayed at the
National Museum of the U.S. Air
Force, near Dayton, Ohio.

On The Nose

Personalizing their aircraft meant a lot to the WW2 bomber crews of the RAF and the USAAF, and they did that through what became known as 'nose art.' Among the most prolific of the aircraft nose artists was Tony Starcer of the 91st Bomb Group. His illustrations on more than 130 B-17s included that of *Memphis Belle*, *Outhouse Mouse*, *Dame Satan*, *Nine O Nine*, *Delta Rebel*, and *Careful Virgin*.

She was pretty. She was built. She was American. So she was the past, and a halfway prayer for the future. I could see her in saddle shoes and a knocked-out sweater and skirt. I could see her sucking on a Coke straw, and I could see her all ruffled up after a long ride home in a rumble seat. She was a symbol of something that was always there, in the back of the mind, or out bright in the foreground, a girl with slim brown shoulders, in a sheer white formal with a flower in her hair, dancing through the night.
—from *Serenade to the Big Bird*, by Bert Stiles

PICTURE CREDITS: PHOTOS FROM THE AUTHOR'S COLLECTION ARE CREDITED: AC; PHOTOS FROM THE U.S. NATIONAL ARCHIVES AND RECORDS ADMINISTRATION ARE CREDITED: NARA; PHOTOS FROM THE IMPERIAL WAR MUSEUM ARE CREDITED: IWM: P3 AC, P4 FAR LEFT-NARA, CENTRE-IWM, RIGHT-AC; P5 TOP RIGHT-AC, BOTTOM-AC; P6-AC, P7-NARA; P8-AC; P9-AC; P10-DE HAVILLAND AIRCRAFT; P11-AC; P13 BOTH-AC; P14 LEFT-M. O'LEARY, RIGHT-NARA; BOTTOM-AC; P15-AC; P16 TOP BOTH AND LEFT-T. FRISSELL/LIBRARY OF CONGRESS, CENTRE AND BOTTOM-AC; PP18-AC; P20-T. FRISSELL/LIBRARY OF CONGRESS; P21-AC; P23 TOP BOTH-AC, BOTTOM-DEGOLYER LIBRARY, SOUTHERN METHODIST UNIVERSITY; P24 BOTH-AC; P25-T. FRISSELL/LIBRARY OF CONGRESS; PP 26-NARA; P29-AC; P30-T. FRISSELL/LIBRARY OF CONGRESS; P32-U.S.A.F. ACADEMY; P33ALL-AC; P34 BOTH-AC; P35-AC; P36-AC; P37 BOTH-AC; P38 BOTH-AC; P39 BOTH-AC; P40-J. FALCONER; P41-J. FALCONER; P42-NARA; P43-T. FRISSELL/LIBRARY OF CONGRESS; P44-R. ARMSTRONG; P45-AC; P47-AC; P48-AC; P49AC; PP50-51 ALL-DE HAVILLAND AIRCRAFT; P52-AC; P53-AC; P54 TOP-AC, BOTTOM-R. WILD; P56 TOP-NARA, BOTTOM-USAF; P57-AC; P58-T. FRISSELL/LIBRARY OF CONGRESS; P59 TOP BOTH-T. FRISSELL/LIBRARY OF CONGRESS, BOTTOM-AC; P60 TOP-T. FRISSELL/LIBRARY OF CONGRESS, BOTTOM-AC; P61-AC; P62-AC; P63-AC; P64 TOP-M. AGAZARIAN, BOTTOM-AC; P65 ALL-AC; P66-AC; P67 TOP-T. FRISSELL/LIBRARY OF CONGRESS, BOTTOM-AC; P68-O. BOESCH; P70 TOP LEFT-AC, TOP RIGHT-A. HENSHAW, BOTTOM-AC; P72 TOP-C.E. BROWN, BOTTOM-AC; P73 ALL-AC; P74-AC; P76 TOP BOTH-AC, BOTTOM-REPUBLIC AVIATION; P77 TOP AND BOTTOM LEFT-M. OLMSTED, BOTTOM RIGHT-DEGOLYER LIBRARY, SOUTHERN METHODIST UNIVERSITY; P79 TOP-AC, BOTTOM-T. FRISSELL/LIBRARY OF CONGRESS; P80 BOTH-AC; P81 BOTH-AC; P83 BOTH-NARA; P84 BOTH-W. MCCARREN; P85-AC; P86-AC; P86 BOTH-AC; P87 BOTH-AC; P90 TOP-AC, BOTTOM-AC; P92 BOTH-AC; P93 BOTH-AC; P94-AC; P95-AC; P96-USAF; P97-USAF; P98-AC; P99-E. ALSTON; P101-R. ARMSTRONG; P102-AC; P104-AC; P106-AC; P107-AC; P108-M. OLMSTED; P110-AC; P112-AC; P113-AC; P114-IWM; P116-AC; P118 BOTH-AC; P119 BOTH-AC; P120-AC; P121 BOTH-AC; P122-AC; P124-AC; P125-AC; P126-AC; P127 BOTH-AC; P128-AC.

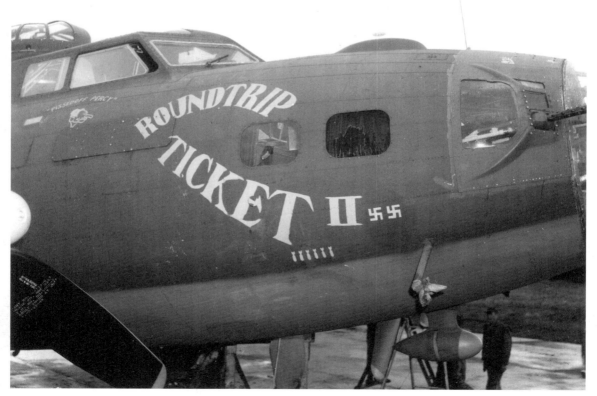